The Samurai

PAGEANT OF HISTORY EDITOR: JOHN GROSS

H. Paul Varley
with Ivan and Nobuko Morris

The Samurai

WEIDENFELD AND NICOLSON 5 WINSLEY STREET LONDON WI.

© 1970 by H. Paul Varley (with Ivan and Nobuko Morris)

SBN 297 00132 9

Printed in Great Britain by Ebenezer Baylis & Son Limited
The Trinity Press, Worcester, and London

To Betty Jane Varley

The word 'samurai' derives from the Japanese verb *saburau*, 'to serve'. Used in earliest times for personal attendants who appear to have been little better than domestic servants, it later came to be applied exclusively to members of a provincial warrior class.

Japanese names: the order is family name first and given name second. Thus Minamoto Yoshiie is Yoshiie of the Minamoto family.

Year-periods: following the Chinese practice, the Japanese of pre-modern times designated 'year-periods' or 'calendrical eras' that lasted, at their discretion, from a period of months to several decades. Important events, such as the Hōgen Incident of 1156 and the Ōnin War (1467–1477), often came to be known by the year-periods in which they occurred or began.

Contents

Acknowledgements

The authors and publishers would like to thank Dr Joseph Shulman for his photographs of the armour in the collection of Ivan Morris and the people and institutional below for permission to reproduce the photographs on the pages mentioned before their names.

17 (top and bottom), Hideo Aoki; 18 (bottom), 19 (top and bottom), Asano Collection, Tokyo; 13, 20 (top), 60, 64 (top and bottom), 78/79, 117 (bottom), British Museum; 37 (bottom), 97 (top), 99 (top), 100, Chikuma Shobo, Tokyo; 54, 63, 73, 77, 85, 117 (bottom), John Freeman and Co.; 37 (top), Goto Art Museum, Tokyo; 20 (bottom), 73 (top and bottom), 74/75, 76, 77, Imperial Household Collection, Kyoto; 98 (bottom), Itsuo Art Museum, Osaka; 80 (top and bottom), Mainichi Newspapers, Tokyo; jacket, 38, 62, 63, Ivan Morris; 58/59, Museum of Fine Arts, Boston, 39 (top), Okura Cultural Foundation, Tokyo; jacket, 38, Dr Joseph Shulman; 97 (bottom), 99 (bottom), Stanford University Press; 57 (top and bottom), Tokyo National Museum; 18 (top), Tuttle Company; 21, 23, 25, 36, 39 (bottom), 40 (top and bottom), 41, 45, 47, 60/61, 61, 90, 95, 117 (top), 118/119, 120, Victoria and Albert Museum; 98 (top), Yoshio Watanabe; 21, 25, 36, 41, 45, 47, 118/119, Derrick Witty.

1
Genesis of government by assassination

A blanket of snow covered Tokyo in the early hours before dawn on 26 February 1936 as more than fourteen hundred troops of the Japanese Army's First Division filed swiftly out of their barracks and moved to occupy positions near the Imperial Palace grounds, including the Diet Building and the Office of the Minister of War. These men, led only by junior officers, were embarked on a desperate and ambitious mission: to overthrow the Government of Japan.

In the same pre-dawn hours other, smaller groups of soldiers also sallied forth. One group went directly to the home of the venerable Admiral Saitō, Lord Keeper of the privy Seal and former Prime Minister, whom they found asleep with his wife on the matted floor of their bedroom. The intruders immediately opened fire on Saitō, brusquely pushing aside his wife when she attempted to protect his body with her own. Mrs Saitō received a bullet wound in her arm; yet, despite her gallant efforts, her husband was riddled with more than thirty rounds, fired at point-blank range.

Another group went in search of Count Makino, a close adviser of the emperor, and found him on a slope behind the country inn where he had been staying. Just as the members of the group were about to shoot, Makino's granddaughter leaped in front of him and held out the sleeves of her kimono protectively. Struck with admiration at this gallant act, the soldiers momentarily paused. Although they subsequently fired and hit another guest of the inn who was helping Makino, knocking both men down, the Count escaped unharmed.

Admiral Okada, the incumbent Prime Minister, was also miraculously saved from the group sent to murder him. As the soldiers entered the official residence of the Prime Minister,

Okada's brother-in-law hid him in a small bathroom usually reserved for servants. The brother-in-law, who bore a striking resemblance to Okada, then confronted the men and virtually invited them to shoot him down. They did, and believed they had got the right man. Two days later, when the body of the 'Prime Minister' was borne away with the permission of the soldiers, who still held the premises, Okada made good his escape, disguised as one of the men in charge of funeral arrangements.

Other victims of that night of terror included the Inspector General of Military Education, General Watanabe, and the Finance Minister (and also former Prime Minister), Mr Takahashi, who was hacked with a sword by one soldier, while another pumped bullets into him.

Hugh Byas, a pre-war foreign correspondent for *The New York Times*, described the political process in Japan of the 1930s as 'government by assassination'. The murders committed during the so-called February Mutiny of 1936 were simply the latest in a series of assassinations of political, military, and business figures dating back to the early years of the decade. In each incident the killers had been right-wing ultranationalists who professed to be acting on behalf of their emperor and for the salvation of Japan. The perpetrators of the February Mutiny, for example, issued a manifesto to the press in which they bitterly denounced the cabinet officials, elder statesmen, and greedy industrialists, whom they saw as responsible for Japan's domestic and international ills. Only by destroying these evil men who monopolized access to the throne would it be possible to bring about a restoration of imperial rule.

Assassins earlier in the 1930s had used the occasion of their trials to explain to the court the purity of their motives. They had been inspired by an overwhelming love of country and adoration for their god-like emperor. Few, if any, had any specific idea of what would happen if the larger plots of political revolution connected with their violent acts were successful. They thought only of destroying and, with extraordinary naïveté, assumed that the emperor would beneficently handle the task of reconstruction. A contemporary Japanese scholar has commented on how the participants in the February Mutiny similarly believed that this was how things would work out:

> . . . the content of their ideology was extremely vague and abstract, being the principle of accepting the absolute authority of the Emperor and submitting humbly to his wishes. One of the reasons that the participants' plans covered only the violent stage of the operation and were not concerned with the aftermath is that their thoughts were based on the principle of the absolute authority of the Emperor. In other words, any attempt at formulating plans of reconstruction would be tantamount to surmising the will of the Emperor and thus an invasion of the Imperial prerogative. This leads to a mythological sort of optimism according to which, if only evil men could be removed from the Court, if only the dark clouds shrouding the Emperor could be swept away, the Imperial sun would naturally shine forth.*

The emperor in whom these activists had such implicit faith was, in fact, a mild-mannered, retiring man with a scholarly interest in marine biology. He lived a remote and guarded existence and offered only occasional advice and opinion to his chief ministers of state. When first informed of the cataclysmic events of the early morning of 26 February, however, the emperor was outraged. He insisted that the 'rebels' be crushed and, in this instance, gave great moral support to army officials in their successful efforts to disperse the insurgent troops during the next few days.

Actually the February Mutiny of 1936 differed from earlier assassination incidents and attempted governmental coups in that it marked the culmination of a bitter factional fight within the Japanese Army. The mutiny was a final attempt by certain extremist young officers to have their radical views accepted by the army. After a group of senior officers, with the emperor's help, broke the mutiny, they brought the ringleaders speedily to trial and, without allowing them to air their sentiments publically, meted out severe punishments, including execution.

* Maruyama Masao. *Thought and Behaviour in Modern Japanese Politics.* Ivan Morris (ed.). London: Oxford University Press, 1963. P. 69.

With the failure of the February Mutiny and the reinstitution of control within the army, the most extreme and overtly violent phase in the internal development of what some scholars have called Japan's pre-war era of fascism came to an end. Henceforth, Japanese violence was to be directed outward in the aggressive foreign policy that ultimately led to the Pacific War.

Yet the sentiments of patriotism that had been expressed by the assassins of the early 1930s and the direct manner in which they acted had strongly appealed to many of their fellow countrymen. Even among those Japanese who most deplored bloodshed there was undoubtedly a certain sympathy for the assassins' behaviour. These men had consciously acted in accordance with an ancient and respected code: that of the samurai warrior of Japan's feudal past. Many of them abhorred the complexities of modern life, with its depersonalizing tendencies, its inculcation of greed, and its stress on the material rather than the spiritual in man's existence. They had a great nostalgia for the kind of society they believed existed in Japan before the intrusion of the West in the mid-nineteenth century, and yearned for a return to its simpler virtues and values. Some were outright agrarian primitivists; others had only a hazy notion about building a new Japan in which they, as twentieth-century samurai, would devote themselves exclusively to the service of the throne.

What precisely is the 'samurai tradition' or 'way of the samurai' which appealed so powerfully to these activists of pre-war Japan? Most commonly it refers to the behavioural pattern of the class of professional warriors who emerged from the provinces of Japan about the tenth or eleventh centuries and who, within another hundred years or so, became the ruling élite of the land, a position they held until Japan entered the modern era in 1868. Yet even more broadly the samurai way or tradition may be said simply to designate the warrior spirit of the Japanese, which has its origins in a much earlier age.

Among the remains found in burial tombs in Japan from about the fourth century AD are large numbers and varieties of weapons and other fighting accoutrements – spears, swords, daggers, shields, body-armour, helmets, bows and arrows, quivers – which

The samurai as symbol of the Japanese warrior spirit, by Hokusai

clearly attest to the highly sophisticated martial orientation of Japanese society even before the dawn of fully recorded history. In addition these tombs have given forth innumerable clay figurines or *haniwa*, usually a few feet high, that depict, among other things, armour-clad warriors, their equipment and their saddled mounts. The warrior *haniwa*, which are often very detailed in their workmanship, collectively give us an invaluable picture of the fighting-man of early Japan. Attired in either a corset-like or full-length suit of armour, his head encased in a bowl-shaped helmet fitted with neck and cheek protectors, and his hand about to unsheath a sword hanging from his waist, the typical sturdy little warrior of these figurines is the very image of military preparedness and *élan*.

Yet the native warrior spirit that apparently flourished in earlier times began to wane in the sixth century as Japan came increasingly under the civilizing influence of China. With China as a model, the Japanese learned how to write Chinese and began to adapt the Chinese written script to their own spoken language; they studied the major tenets of Buddhism and Confucianism; they created an elaborate civil bureaucracy on Chinese lines; and they imitated the vastly superior arts and culture of China. So industriously did the Japanese labour to reshape their country that by the eighth century they had succeeded in forming a surprisingly similar replica, in miniature, of the grand Chinese Empire of East Asia.

The centre of Japanese government was the imperial court, which was in the city of Nara during the eighth century, and in Heian or Kyoto some twenty-six miles to the north from the ninth century on. Theoretically the power of the Japanese throne was absolute, both politically and sacerdotally, based on the myth that the emperor was directly descended from the supreme Shinto deity, the Sun Goddess. In practice others often arrogated the emperor's political prerogatives. One reason the imperial line has lasted so long is that ambitious families throughout Japanese history have found it expedient to use the throne to legitimize their positions after each had achieved national power.

During the late seventh and eighth centuries the court sought to rule the country efficiently by employing a large officialdom and by maintaining a national army conscripted from the peasantry. But from about the end of this period the various ministerial families that, along with the imperial family, comprised Japan's aristocracy gradually carved up much of the land that had formerly constituted the public domain into their own private estates.

By the Heian period (794–1185) the court, more and more deprived of its tax income as land everywhere fell into private hands, was obliged to curtail many of its former administrative services and to transfer to local militia the responsibility for maintaining order in the provinces. It was this transference of military initiative from the central government to the various localities and regions of Japan that provided the chief impetus for the rise of a provincial warrior class during the tenth and eleventh centuries. Unable to rely on the central government for support, provincial families were obliged to take up arms to provide for their own policing and defence needs.

Although the court declined grievously as a national administrative body during the Heian epoch, it rose to great heights as a cultural centre. From about the middle of the ninth century one ministerial family, the Fujiwara, steadily consolidated its position next to the throne and by the following century was able completely to dominate it from the office of imperial regent. In their heyday the Fujiwara regents married the young girls of their family to emperors and placed the offspring from these unions on the throne. They usually installed emperors at very tender ages and forced them to abdicate before reaching maturity.

Moulding Chinese culture to their own tastes, the Fujiwara fashioned a brilliant civilization in Kyoto. By withdrawing from all but the most unavoidable contacts with the rest of the country, they sought to create a world of pure aesthetic perfection, a world of beauty, poetry and love. Concerned, moreover, only that the revenues continued to flow uninterruptedly from their outlying estates, they showed a grand disregard for provincial affairs.

Yet the provinces were inexorably following their own course of development. In the early tenth century the Heian courtiers were alarmed and bewildered to learn of the uprising of an eastern chieftain named Taira Masakado, who temporarily brought under his sway most of the eight eastern provinces and even had the temerity to proclaim himself the 'new emperor' of Japan. Almost simultaneously, an outlaw of the Fujiwara family, named Sumitomo, became engaged in piracy in the Inland Sea and soon threatened the river-ways that led from the Sea to the capital. Although Masakado and Sumitomo were put down in the early 940s by other chieftains acting under commissions from the throne, their lawless behaviour was the first ominous warning that the court could not remain aloof from affairs in the rest of the land and expect indefinitely to retain its ruling position.

The Kantō and the provinces to the north of it still constituted the frontier of Japan during the early Heian period. For many centuries the court had sought to extend its control ever farther eastward. In the late eighth and early ninth centuries armies commissioned by the court conducted a number of arduous campaigns against wild eastern tribesmen known as Emishi, who were probably of the same ethnic stock as the Japanese but, because of their cultural backwardness, were regarded as distinct outsiders or aliens. Although a settlement was finally achieved with the Emishi which set a boundary in the northern reaches of Honshu and eliminated these tribesmen as a serious threat to the Japanese state, the provinces of the north remained a troublesome area throughout the Heian period. The chief problem in the later centuries, however, was not so much with the Emishi as it was with the officials appointed by the court to watch over them. These provincial officials and their families constantly flouted the court's will and sought to carve out autonomous baronies for themselves in the north. During the course of two protracted wars fought there in the late eleventh century, the northern provinces became a testing-ground for the skills and spirit of the samurai class of warriors who had begun to appear as principal actors in Japanese history from at least the time of the Masakado and Sumitomo rebellions.

Leadership of emerging samurai society, paradoxical as it may at first sound, was assumed mainly by distant relatives of

above: 26 February, 1936. The young rebel soldiers march by the Diet building in the snow.

below: 26 February, 1936. The end of a 'four day nightmare' as the rebels return to their barracks.

Warrior *haniwa*.

Bow stringing (from a thirteenth-century scroll): the stringing of great samurai bows of this type required the strength of several men.

above : Training in the art of war (thirteenth century).

below : Samurai bows in action (thirteenth century).

above : A seventeenth-century samurai prepares to disembowel himself; this was a privilege reserved for members of the warrior class. A French print.

below : After the battle the conqueror is shown the severed heads of his enemies.

the imperial family itself. Since emperors had at their disposal many wives, concubines and other court ladies, they usually produced large progenies. In order to avoid the costly burden of too many imperial relatives, it became necessary over the years to eliminate the more remotely descended. When setting the latter adrift, the throne commonly granted them one of two special surnames – either Minamoto or Taira – and, additionally, appointed them to governorships or other high posts in the provinces. From the tenth century on we hear more and more about the activities of the Minamoto and the Taira: Taira Masakado was simply the earliest to become nationally famous. Although the court regarded him as a rebel, many people in the east viewed Masakado with favour as one who would not bow supinely to Kyoto. Clearly the provinces were looking for their own leaders to remedy the long neglect of the central government.

Lineage was unquestionably one of the most important factors in the success of the Minamoto and the Taira. Even rustic boors of pre-modern times in Japan looked with awe upon those who were graced with high, to say nothing of, royal birth. The Minamoto and Taira were in exceptionally favourable positions to rise above the local chieftains and to become the great overlords of samurai society.

The wars fought in the north during the eleventh century are known, rather unpoetically, as the Former Nine Years War and the Later Three Years War. In 1051 Minamoto Yoriyoshi, at the direction of the court, undertook the Former Nine Years War to restore imperial authority in the province of Dewa, where the Abe family had long held virtually independent sway. Undoubtedly the Abe needed some chastising; but there is good reason to believe also that Yoriyoshi pressed his campaign as hard as he could in order to expand the private power of the Minamoto. The feeling that the Minamoto were using the north as an arena to satisfy their own ambitions was further intensified a few decades later when Yoriyoshi's son, Minamoto Yoshiie, sought to subdue another family in Dewa, the Kiyowara.

With these two eleventh century wars the story of the samurai in Japanese history truly begins. In discussing the ethos and behaviour of these warriors of the mid-Heian epoch one wonders to what extent they were the inheritors of that ancient fighting spirit reflected in the *haniwa* figurines of prehistoric times. Perhaps that spirit was never fully extinguished in the provinces, despite the evolution of a Sinicized court at the head of a national government that stressed the art of persuasion rather than force.

If we are to believe the chronicles of the eleventh century, the true warrior of that age held his life to be of 'no more value than a feather'. Not only was he prepared at all times to die unflinchingly in battle, but he rejected any chance for survival that necessitated turning his back on the enemy. Odds, we are told, meant nothing to him; he was ready to rush into the hottest conflict or to charge the greatest concentration of the enemy if honour and the circumstances of battle so dictated.

In point of fact, the early samurai usually fought individually against one opponent at a time, so that a typical field of battle was more likely to resemble a grouping of separate combats than a general struggle between two armies. Not until much later – about the fourteenth and fifteenth centuries – did the Japanese develop anything beyond the most rudimentary techniques of troop movements and coordinated military manoeuvres.

There is at least one non-technological reason for this relative tardiness in the evolution of mass rather than individual tactics in pre-modern Japanese warfare. Althouth he owed a kind of allegiance to the commanding general of his army, the samurai's particular loyalty was to his immediate overlord. This overlord-follower relationship was already very close to a feudal type of lord-vassal tie, which it became during the medieval age that began a century later. Such a tie was in no sense one-sided. In return for the loyalty and service he rendered his lord, the vassal expected both protection and reward. He preferred to fight alone and to engage in personal heroics in order to impress his lord and to secure as large a share as possible of the rewards that victory would bring.

In a pre-modern agricultural society where the principal form of wealth was land, by far the most important rewards were land or the claim to income from it. Nearly all battles in the military centuries of Japanese history were therefore fought for land and usually the chief, if not the only, aim in each conflict was to confiscate the holdings of the enemy for redistribution among the victors. The derivation of a common phrase in modern Japanese, *issho kemmei*, which means 'desperately' or 'frantically', can even be traced to the early samurai's zeal to acquire landed property. An ancient combination of written characters, *issho kemmei* has the literal sense of 'to risk one's life for a place (or a holding of land)' on this earth.

One characteristic practice of the lone-fighting Japanese warrior was that of name-calling or 'pronouncement of pedigree'. Preparatory to combat it was usual for the samurai to declaim to his potential opponents something like this: 'I am Yoshikiyo of the Minamoto clan, grandson of Tomokiyo, the former deputy governor of Musashi Province, and son of Yorikiyo, who distinguished himself in various battles in the northern territories. I myself am of little personal merit and I care not whether I live or die in today's conflict. So if any of you would like to test my strength of arms, come forth now'. Such pronouncements, apart from their stereotyped tone of bravado and false humility, are good proof of the samurai's fierce pride in his lineage and family background.

Indeed the samurai fought less for himself than for his family and its perpetuation. He was prepared to forfeit his life in battle, if necessary, in the conviction that his family would benefit from the rewards his sacrifice would bring. So important were family bonds and the sense of family solidarity that even where these bonds did not exist they were often fictively assumed. Thus we find lords referring to their vassals by such terms as 'housemen' (*ke'nin*) and 'children of the household' (*ie no ko*) and followers looking upon their masters as second fathers.

The chronicles record many instances in which older warriors or lords lectured younger samurai at length to ignore all worldly attachments when in battle, insisting, for example, that brothers be prepared to ride over the corpses of brothers and sons over those of their fathers. Yet in fact the samurai was often torn by loyalty to his lord on the one hand and desire for reward on the other. There are many examples of samurai who remained true in the face of all adversity. At the same time there are more than sufficient cases of outright treachery and transference of allegiance from one side to the other, even in the midst of battle, to disabuse us of any notion that samurai warfare was all gallantry and high conduct. During the civil struggles that raged throughout the land in the fourteenth century, members of the same family often joined opposing forces simply to be represented on the winning side no matter how the fighting went.

Even in earliest times the samurai's code seems to have called for an exaggerated sense of personal pride and 'face', which as often as not manifested itself in swaggering, bullying behaviour towards others. Undoubtedly such behaviour was a natural and even psychologically necessary concomitant to the warrior profession. Nevertheless the samurai's overweening pride often caused him to act in a manner utterly contrary to reason and good sense. This can be illustrated by an incident which occurred during the Later Three Years War. In a certain battle a youthful warrior named Kagemasa, who was a bare sixteen years of age, was shot in the left eye. With the arrow shaft still protruding from his face, he closed with and destroyed his adversary. One of Kagemasa's allies, Tametsugu, attempted to aid the fallen boy by placing his sandalled foot against Kagemasa's cheek to withdraw the arrow. In great indignation Kagemasa leaped up and declared that, while he was prepared as a samurai to die from an arrow wound, so long as he lived he would allow no man to put a foot on his face. So saying, he even attempted in his rage to cut down the hapless Tametsugu.

The chief skills which the samurai sought to cultivate were horsemanship and archery. Indeed, in the legends of early warrior society the way of the samurai was known simply as the way of the 'bow and the horse'. The eastern samurai were in particular arrogantly proud of their ability to ride and shoot arrows. In the still frontier-like and culturally unsophisticated provinces of the east, the future warrior grew up on horseback and learned from an early age how to use a bow that purportedly required the strength of several men to bend and string, and arrows that were some fourteen to fifteen hand-breadths in length. The mounted samurai who fought in the northern campaigns of the late eleventh century also carried a sword into battle, although he did not rely upon it nearly as much as upon his bow since the sword of that time was straight and rather unwieldly for close in-fighting. Not until the following century did the Japanese evolve the curved sword, which then became the chief combat weapon for the individual samurai.

Two of the most famous samurai swords were, however, products of the tenth century and became prized heirlooms of successive heads of the Minamoto clan. These were known as the

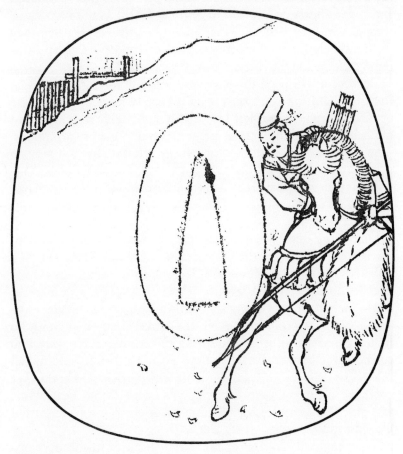

Mounted samurai with bow and arrows: early nineteenth-century design for a sword-guard

'beard-cutter' and the 'knee-cutter' from the purported fact that each was of such a sharpness that, when used to decapitate a kneeling person, it not only cut through his neck but through his beard and knees as well.

In later centuries an elaborate mystique evolved about the forging, possession and use of swords. Japan's master-sword-smiths created their steel blades under highly ritualistic conditions, and the best of these were often believed by samurai owners to have an inherent spiritual quality of their own. The extreme reverence in which the ancient samurai held their swords induced Japanese officers as late as the Second World War to lug these weapons with their heavy scabbards into battle even when they were unlikely to be of much practical use in a type of hand-to-hand combat fought chiefly with bayoneted rifles.

Because of his need for great physical mobility on horseback, the early samurai wore only a light type of protective clothing or 'armour' which still left him highly vulnerable in many areas of his body to a skilfully shot arrow or a well-aimed sword thrust. The more elaborate kinds of Japanese armour that are seen in museums and collections are products of a much later age – the sixteenth or early seventeenth centuries – when warfare had become far more regimented and mobility could be sacrificed for greater protection.

One thing that must strike anyone who examines sets of Japanese armour from the medieval period is how small the men must have been who wore them. It has only been in the past few decades that dietary changes have brought a dramatic increase in the height of the Japanese, historically a small people compared to most other races. At the same time it should be remembered that Europeans during the Middle Ages were also considerably shorter than their descendants today. It is estimated that the average height of the knights who participated in the first crusade, just a few years after Japan's Later Three Years War, was only five foot three or four inches. Richard the Lionhearted was considered a giant at six feet.

The mounted samurai of the early centuries in the development of Japan's warrior class was generally accompanied into battle by one or two grooms on foot. These grooms did not par-

Kuniyoshi: ceremonial forging of a sword, attended by the Fox-spirit

ticipate in the actual fighting, but rather aided their masters personally by carrying their equipment and by performing such functions as the gathering of enemy heads, which were necessary for later identification and distribution of rewards. Only with the passage of several hundred years did the true, spear-carrying foot soldier first make his appearance in Japan. Soldiers on foot and armed with a kind of long sword (*naginata*), which in fact looked very much like a sharpened hockey stick, do appear frequently in the picture scrolls depicting eleventh-century warfare; but there is nothing in the written records to suggest that these soldiers were used in any organized or large-scale manner. The individual samurai on horseback was to remain supreme in warfare for some time to come and was never, for a variety of reasons to be explained, fully replaced even with the increasing mobilization of troops in the middle and late medieval periods.

Fighting among the samurai of the eleventh and twelfth centuries was to a surprising degree governed by formal and exacting standards of procedure. The battle, for example, was usually arranged through an exchange of messengers employed to decide upon an appropriate time and site for action. It is recorded that on one occasion a commanding general was so displeased with the wording of an enemy's message that he had the messenger who bore it killed. To the general's chagrin this breach of 'civilized' behaviour thoroughly dispirited his own soldiers and they were either unable or unwilling to fight effectively for him.

Perhaps the most dramatic moment in the preliminaries to battle arrived after the two armies had aligned themselves and a leading stalwart from each side advanced to do the principal name calling. In a loud and fierce voice each proclaimed his lineage and the great achievements of his ancestors and expounded upon the justness of his army's cause. The aim was to buoy the spirits of the ally and to intimidate the foe. After both had finished, two 'humming arrows' were sent aloft to signal the commencement of a general exchange of arrows. The direction of the wind and other factors of weather, terrain and angle of trajectory helped determine which of the two sides gained the advantage at this time. In order to get off better shots, the bolder samurai moved forward – frequently to a range of fifty yards or closer – where real accuracy with the bow was possible. Finally, when the moment seemed right or the supply of arrows on both sides was running short, the armies charged.

The task of the individual samurai in the charge was to find a worthy opponent – that is, an opponent of comparable rank and merit – with whom to do combat. There must have been considerable confusion as the various warriors milled about shouting their qualifications. Once paired off, however, the samurai began

Samurai and retainer, Tosa school

to slash with their swords. The aim of each was not so much to deal a mortal blow, which would have been difficult in any case from horseback, as to stun and unseat the other. As soon as this was achieved, the samurai would leap down from his own horse to grapple with his opponent and to administer the death stab with a short dagger he carried at his waist for that purpose.

The post-battle activities included a great victory shout and the counting of heads to determine who had accomplished what.

Often the heads of grooms and other low-ranking persons disguised as samurai were found among the victor's collections and these, of course, had to be excluded from the final count. An embarrassing possibility was the discovery also of one or two 'allied' or 'friendly' heads. A common punishment meted out to a samurai guilty of erroneously acquiring one of these was the severance of a finger, usually from the right hand.

Heads of generals or famous warriors taken by troops commissioned by the court were almost always transported back to the capital to be displayed before officials and the populace. A poignant tale is told about the delivery of the head of the rebel leader, Abe Sadatō, to Kyoto after the Former Nine Years War. An accompanying porter asked one of the guards to lend him a comb so he could dress his dead master's hair. When the guard curtly told him to use his own comb, the porter, weeping bitterly, said: 'When my master was alive I looked up to him as to heaven. How could I ever have imagined that I would be forced to dress his hair with this filthy comb of mine?'

Even as early as the mid-twelfth century, however, the old ways of 'civilized' warfare seem to have begun to wane. Far from organized and carefully staged battles, surprise or sneak attacks became more and more common. Veteran warriors lamented that younger samurai ignored the honourable rules of conduct by deliberately aiming their arrows at horses and by seeking only to catch their adversaries off guard. If these laments did indeed indicate significant changes in methods of warfare, this was probably largely the result of the greatly increased scale of fighting from about the middle of the twelfth century in Japan.

Inasmuch as the samurai were offered special rewards for taking the initiative in battle, they often went to great and even farcical lengths to be the first to engage the foe. It was not at all unusual, for example, for a samurai to steal out of camp at night and move forward to an advanced position in order to ride ahead of the others in an attack planned for the following morning. It was also not unusual for such a samurai to find that one or more of his comrades in arms had similar ideas and were during the same night trying to move even farther ahead than he.

One of the most famous instances of competition to be first occurred during the battle of the Uji River in the warfare of the 1180s between the Minamoto and the Taira that ushered in the medieval age. A captain of the Minamoto armies, Hatakeyama Shigetada, rode into the waters of the Uji River before all the others. And even when his horse was struck by an arrow shot from the Taira position on the opposite bank, Shigetada swam the remaining distance. As he started to pull himself ashore, he felt someone tugging at him and saw that it was a samurai he knew named Shigechika, who pleaded that he had not the strength to make it by himself. But when Shigetada took hold of him and tossed him onto the bank, Shigechika immediately sprang to his feet and proclaimed that he was the first to cross the Uji River. In fact, neither of these men was first: two other samurai who entered at another part of the stream received this honour, which was duly recorded in the Minamoto annals and was undoubtedly recounted by their descendants on innumerable occasions of their own name-callings in later centuries.

A common feature of samurai life through the ages was the vendetta, which was especially encouraged by the widely-held injunction that the true samurai must never be content to live under the same heaven with the slayer of his father or his lord. Curiously the Japanese never developed any true institutional devices for handling or precluding the vendetta, such as the German *Wergeld* whereby a person who slew or maimed another was ordered to pay a sum of money to the latter or his family. In early Germanic society most persons and even parts of the body came to have their separate *Wergeld* evaluations; that is, different sums were due for the killing of a nobleman or a freeman, and for the loss of an arm, an eye and so forth.

The most famous of all Japanese vendettas was undertaken by forty-seven *rōnin*, or 'masterless samurai,' in the early 1700s; but countless others also appear in the annals of Japanese history. A grisly consequence of fear of the vendetta was that the samurai leader, after destroying an enemy, usually attempted to round up as many of the latter's relatives and close retainers as possible and to put them to the sword to prevent any later undertaking of a crusade of vengeance.

A special feature of the unwritten samurai code, and one that holds a particularly morbid fascination for foreigners, was the obligation which the samurai was expected to assume under certain circumstances to commit suicide, which he usually chose to do by means of disembowelment.

Examples of suicide can be traced to the earliest records of the Japanese. One especially gruesome method, apparently practised from remote times, was that of allowing oneself to be buried alive in order to join a lord in death. The precise origins of disembowelment as the samurai's preferred method of self-destruction are unknown, although the practice appears to have evolved with warrior society itself in the middle and later years of the Heian period. Disembowelment was performed on a number of occasions during the struggles between the Taira and the Minamoto in the late twelfth century and may even have been carried out in one or two isolated instances during the northern campaigns of the Minamoto in the latter half of the eleventh century.

The two words most commonly used to designate this peculiarly Japanese form of suicide are: the formal term of *seppuku*, or 'disembowelment'; and the more vulgar expression of *hara-kiri*, or 'belly-slitting', which is widely known in the West. Whichever term is used, disembowelment became the samurai's special way of taking his life with honour and indeed this form of suicide appears so frequently in the war tales of the medieval centuries that one is surprised to read more than a few pages or a chapter of one of these tales without encountering it.

In the tumultuous early centuries of samurai history disembowelment was performed under various circumstances: to avoid capture in battle, which the samurai not only believed to be dishonourable and degrading but generally bad policy, since prisoners were often tortured and otherwise wretchedly treated; to atone for a misdeed or an unworthy act; and, perhaps most interestingly, to admonish one's lord.

One of the most striking differences between the Japanese samurai and the Western knight lay in their respective attitudes towards capture by the enemy. There was nothing in the latter's code that cast opprobrium on capture under honourable conditions. Seizure and incarceration could on occasion even enhance a knight's reputation, as they did Richard the Lionhearted's when he blundered into the custody of the German emperor, Henry VI, while on his way home from the third crusade. The captured European knight looked for courteous and considerate treatment and his vassals were usually expected to raise the ransom for his release as part of their feudal obligations.

In the medieval European tournament or joust, moreover, the principal object was to 'capture' opponents by unseating them from their horses. William Marshal, Richard's distinguished contemporary, became a wealthy man by holding for 'ransom' the innumerable chevaliers he managed to defeat in simulated combat.

The Japanese, on the other hand, held few things in greater contempt than capture or surrender, and it came to be universally expected of warriors that they be prepared to destroy themselves to avoid falling into enemy hands. If taken alive they could only anticipate brutal treatment.

The responsibility felt by the early samurai to call his lord's attention respectfully to any errors or shortcomings in the lord's behaviour was strongly endorsed by Confucian tenets. If frank advice or direct petitions failed to bring results, the samurai retainer occasionally resorted to disembowelment to bring his lord to his senses. One of the most famous cases of 'admonitory disembowelment' occurred in the late sixteenth century shortly before the great general, Oda Nobunaga, began the process of military consolidation which unified Japan after nearly a century of anarchy. Nobunaga, by nature a man of violence, was during his youth particularly wild and unmanageable. When all attempts to divert him from his obstreperous ways failed, a retainer, who had long served the Oda family, finally committed suicide. It is recounted that this selfless act so impressed Nobunaga that he began immediately to assume the responsibilities and to undertake the training that were eventually to lead to military greatness.

Nobunaga's successor as military hegemon of Japan was Toyotomi Hideyoshi. On one occasion Hideyoshi agreed to a truce with an opposing chieftain if the chieftain's samurai

lieutenant, who had been in command of the advance fortifica-
tion that Hideyoshi had been investing, committed *seppuku*.
When this was agreed upon, another samurai, who was a vassal
of the man condemned to death, requested that his master come
to his apartment so that he could assure him that disembowelment was not particularly difficult to do. To prove his point, the
underling opened his robes to reveal that he had already cut open
his own stomach.

From the seventeenth century, after warfare had ceased, disembowelment became the usual death sentence imposed upon
the samurai found guilty of a capital offence. The act, for which
we have many detailed accounts, was normally performed by
stabbing a knife into the left side of the abdomen, drawing it
across to the right and giving a final upward twist towards the
chest cavity. By some it came to be considered an appropriate
gesture of bravado or defiance to draw out part of the entrails and
to leave them hanging from the wound. Since death was not fast
in coming even if one cut deeply into the stomach, it soon
became the practice to engage a 'second' to administer a sword
blow that would end the suffering. This meant that the performer squatted down cross-legged, ripped open his stomach and
then stretched out his neck to allow the second to decapitate him.
The task of the second was not an easy one, since it required a
sharp blade and great skill to behead a person who was in a
squatting or kneeling position. Ideally, the second did not cut
entirely through the neck, but left just enough flesh and skin to
hold the head to the body and to prevent it from rolling grotes-
quely away. It was also the second's responsibility to watch for
anything that might suggest fear or cowardice on the part of the
performer and to levy the final blow immediately to preserve the
man's honour in death.

During the Tokugawa period (1600–1867), when Japan
enjoyed more than two and a half centuries of almost uninterrupted peace, *seppuku* became a highly formalized and ritualized
act. It was also abbreviated, in many cases, to eliminate the
excruciating task of actually thrusting a dagger into the stomach.
No honour was deemed lost, for example, if one simply scratched
or cut the skin slightly and then immediately allowed the second

to wield his sword. Nevertheless, there were some samurai quite
late in the Tokugawa period, and even after, who chose to disembowel themselves in the traditional fashion. A. B. Mitford, an
early Secretary to the British Consulate of Japan, has recorded in
vivid detail in his *Tales of Old Japan* an act of *seppuku*, which he
witnessed, that was performed in 1868:

> The condemned man was Taki Zenzaburô, an officer of the
> Prince of Bizen, who gave the order to fire upon the foreign
> settlement at Hiogo in the month of February 1868 . . .

> The ceremony, which was ordered by the Mikado himself,
> took place at 10.30 at night in the temple of Seifukuji, the head-
> quarters of the Satsuma troops at Hiogo. A witness was sent
> from each of the foreign legations. We were seven foreigners
> in all.

> We were conducted to the temple by the officers of the
> Princes of Satsuma and Choshiu. Although the ceremony was
> to be conducted in the most private manner, the casual remarks
> which we overheard in the streets, and a crowd lining the
> principal entrance to the temple, showed that it was a matter of
> no little interest to the public. The courtyard of the temple
> presented a most picturesque sight; it was crowded with
> soldiers standing about in knots round large fires, which threw
> dim flickering light over the heavy eaves and quaint gable-ends
> of the sacred buildings. We were shown into an inner room,
> where we were to wait until the preparation for the ceremony
> was completed: in the next room to us were the high Japanese
> officers. After a long interval, which seemed doubly long from
> the silence which prevailed, Ito Shunské, the provisional
> Governor of Hiogo, came and took down our names, and in-
> formed us that seven *kenshi*, sheriffs or witnesses, would
> attend on the part of the Japanese. He and another officer
> represented the Mikado; two captains of Satsuma's infantry,
> and two of Choshiu's with a representative of the Prince of
> Bizen, the clan of the condemned man, completed the number,
> which was probably arranged in order to tally with that of

the foreigners. Ito Shunské further inquired whether we wished to put any questions to the prisoner. We replied in the negative.

A further delay then ensued, after which we were invited to follow the Japanese witnesses into the *hondo* or main hall of the temple, where the ceremony was to be performed. It was an imposing scene. A large hall with a high roof supported by dark pillars of wood. From the ceiling hung a profusion of those huge gilt lamps and ornaments peculiar to Buddhist temples. In front of the high altar, where the floor, covered with beautiful white mats, is raised some three or four inches from the ground, was laid a rug of scarlet felt. Tall candles placed at regular intervals gave out a dim mysterious light, just sufficient to let all the proceedings be seen. The seven Japanese took their places on the left of the raised floor, the seven foreigners on the right. No other person was present.

After an interval of a few minutes of anxious suspense, Taki Zenzaburô, a stalwart man, thirty-two years of age, with a noble air, walked into the hall attired in his dress of ceremony, with the peculiar hempen-cloth wings which are worn on great occasions. He was accompanied by a *kaishaku* and three officers, who wore the *jimbaori* or war surcoat with gold-tissue facings. The word *kaishaku*, it should be observed, is one to which our word '*executioner*' is no equivalent term. The office is that of a gentleman: in many cases it is performed by a kinsman or friend of the condemned, and the relation between them is rather that of principal and second than that of victim and executioner. In this instance the *kaishaku* was a pupil of Taki Zenzaburô, and was selected by the friends of the latter from among their own number for his skill in swordsmanship.

With the *kaishaku* on his left hand, Taki Zenzaburô advanced slowly towards the Japanese witnesses, and the two bowed before them, then drawing near to the foreigners they saluted us in the same way, perhaps even with more deference: in each case the salutation was ceremoniously returned.

above : Scene of Heian court life (from a twelfth-century scroll): the samurai strove to emulate the aestheticism of the Heian courtiers.

below : A samurai saddle elaborately inlaid with mother-of-pearl.

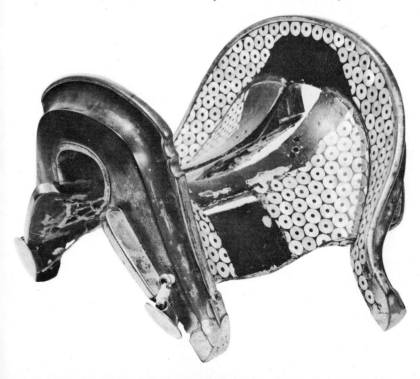

A samurai in full ceremonial armour; his metal face-mask accurately copied his features so that he could be recognized in battle.

above : A swordsmith polishing a sword (sixteenth century).

below : Two samurai engage in sword-play (nineteenth-century colour print by Kuniyoshi illustrating a popular Kabuki drama).

above : Two samurai race each other across the river at the battle of Ujigawa (1184). The first across will get all the glory.

left : A nineteenth-century sword-guard depicting the race of the rival generals across the Uji river.

Slowly, and with great dignity, the condemned man mounted
on to the raised floor, prostrated himself before the high altar
twice, and seated himself on the felt carpet with his back to
the high altar, the *kaishaku* crouching on his left-hand side.
One of the three attendant officers then came forward, bearing
a stand of the kind used in temples for offerings, on which,
wrapped in paper, lay the *wakizashi*, the short sword or dirk of
the Japanese, nine inches and a half in length, with a point and
an edge as sharp as a razor's. This he handed, prostrating
himself, to the condemned man, who received it reverently,
raising it to his head with both hands, and placed it in front of
himself.

After another profound obeisance, Taki Zenzaburô, in a
voice which betrayed so much emotion and hesitation as
might be expected from a man who is making a painful con-
fession, but with no sign of either in his face or manner, spoke
as follows:

"I, and I alone, unwarrantably gave the order to fire on the
foreigners at Kobe, and again as they tried to escape. For this
crime I disembowel myself, and I beg you who are present to
do me the honour of witnessing the act."

Bowing once more, the speaker allowed his upper garments
to slip down to his girdle, and remained naked to the waist.
Carefully, according to custom, he tucked his sleeves under
his knees to prevent himself from falling forwards. Deliberately, with a steady hand, he took the dirk that lay before him;
he looked at it wistfully, almost affectionately; for a moment
seemed to collect his thoughts for the last time, and then,
stabbing himself deeply below the waist on the left-hand side,
he drew the dirk slowly across to the right side, and, turning
it in the wound, gave a slight cut upwards. During this
sickeningly painful operation he never moved a muscle of his
face. When he drew out the dirk, he leaned forward and stretched out his neck; an expression of pain for the first time
crossed his face, but he uttered no sound. At that moment the

3

kaishaku, who, still crouching by his side, had been keenly watching his every movement, sprang to his feet, poised his sword for a second in the air; there was a flash, a heavy, ugly thud, a crashing fall; with one blow the head had been severed from the body.

A dead silence followed, broken only by the hideous noise of the blood throbbing out of the inert heap before us, which but a moment before had been a brave and chivalrous man. It was horrible.*

The great hero of the eleventh century campaigns in the north was Minamoto Yoshiie, known also as Hachiman Tarō, or the 'firstborn son of the war god Hachiman'. A contemporary chronicle records that this redoubtable chieftain shot arrows 'like a god', that with a single shaft he could pierce three coats of armour. He appears, without question, to have been an extraordinary leader in a time of hard fighting in a remote and inhospitable region. One legend recounts that on a certain occasion in mid-winter he warmed his half-frozen followers with his own body; another that he spared the life of an enemy captain who lay helplessly before him when the latter was able to reply in verse to a snatch of poetry that Yoshiie recited as he took aim with his bow. A similar poetic exchange between two samurai antagonists of the fifteenth century is recorded by the late Dr Inazo Nitobe in *Bushido, The Soul of Japan*, a book published some years ago which in style and content can today most charitably be called quaint:

> It passes current among us (Japanese) as a piece of authentic history that as Ota Dokan, the great builder of the castle of Tokyo, was pierced through with a spear, his assassin, knowing the poetical predilection of his victim, accompanied his thrust with this couplet:

*A. B. Mitford. *Tales of Old Japan*. Vol I. London: Macmillan 1871. Pp. 231–236.

> Ah! how in moments like these
> Our heart doth grudge the light of life;

whereupon the expiring hero, not one whit daunted by the mortal wound in his side, added the lines:

> Had not in hours of peace,
> It learned to lightly look on life.*

The special courtier-like quality of aesthetic sensibility which Yoshiie was believed to have possessed in addition to his warrior prowess and compassion appealed greatly to Japan's emerging warrior society as it shaped its legendary heroes. We can have little doubt that the vast majority of the provincial military were brutish and rough men with little learning or refinement. Yet collectively they stood in boundless awe of the cultural and artistic achievements of the small class of Heian courtiers whose existence as a ruling élite they threatened and were eventually to destroy. Even in later centuries, when the emperor and his remaining ministers had been reduced to political impotency and, in many cases, to real financial distress, the newly-risen warrior hegemons of the land continued to covet courtly titles and to cherish for themselves the elegant accomplishments of an earlier age that had abhorred violence and the military life.

One of the most intriguing features of the samurai character was the merger of the aesthetic and the killer instincts. Yoshiie's recitation of poetry on the verge of executing a rival commander has been observed. Even the brutal Oda Nobunaga, the sixteenth century unifier, on the occasion of one of his most fateful battles, danced gracefully with a fan in front of his troops just before leading them to the attack. These aesthetic gestures on the part of men like Yoshiie and Nobunaga, as well as the forms of social etiquette rigidly maintained by the samurai, especially in the dark centuries of the later medieval age, became almost indispensable for preventing Japanese society from descending into the abyss of utter barbarism.

The spirit and style of the samurai of medieval times was also strongly influenced by Zen Buddhism, which was introduced to

* Inazo Nitobe. *Bushido, The Soul of Japan.* New York and London: Putnam. 1905. Pp. 33-34.

Page from a book of designs for sword-furniture, 1820

Japan from China about the end of the twelfth century. Zen, which means 'meditation', stresses cultivation of the intuitive faculties and places a high premium on discipline and self-control. It rejects rational decision-making as artificial and delusory, and insists that action must come from emotion. As such, Zen proved particularly congenial to the medieval samurai, who lived with violence and imminent death and who sought to develop such things as 'spontaneity of conduct' and a 'tranquility of heart' to meet the rigours of his profession. Under the influence of Zen, later samurai theorists especially asserted that the true warrior must be constantly prepared to make the ultimate sacrifice of his life in the service of his lord – without a moment's reflection or conscious consideration.

Yoshiie's military successes and the acclaim that he received from the samurai of the eastern and northern provinces came to be viewed with increasing alarm by Kyoto. The court accused Yoshiie of undertaking the Later Three Years War as a private campaign to extend his own influence and refused to grant him economic or financial support. As a consequence, the Minamoto chieftain was obliged to maintain and reward his men out of his own pocket. Yet even as he did so others clamoured to commend their lands to him for protection and to pledge themselves personally as fighting men in his service.

One of the reasons why the Heian nobles, so engrossed in their world of gentle pursuits and palace intrigues, had been able to hold their position as central rulers of Japan for as long as they did was the skill with which they used the provincial samurai as their armed retainers and paid bullies. Michinaga, the greatest of the Fujiwara regents who ruled supreme at the turn of the eleventh century, once referred to the Minamoto as his 'claws and teeth'. From this remark and from other evidence we know that the Fujiwara even during Michinaga's time relied heavily on warriors like the Minamoto to settle their quarrels and to do their strong-arm work.

Although obliged to turn increasingly to them for military support, the Fujiwara and other courtier families made little attempt to conceal the low esteem in which they held the samurai socially. Few ruling élites in history have been as self-conscious of their social and cultural superiority as the courtiers of Heian Japan. From their elegant world of the capital they regarded the provinces as a bleak wilderness and its occupants as uncultured boors. Even a person with otherwise excellent qualifications of lineage and training who had had the misfortune of having been born in the provinces was likely to find most avenues of advancement and acceptance closed to him at court.

The samurai, even in the late eleventh century, seem meekly to have accepted the social opprobrium imposed upon them. In scrolls from the period we see them squatting humbly behind their courtier masters, not yet fully conscious of the burgeoning power that was within a century to propel them to national leadership. The first to intrude upon the authority of the Fujiwara regents were, in fact, not the provincial samurai at all, but members of the imperial family.

About the same time that the Minamoto were pacifying the northern provinces, the first emperor since the ninth century who did not have a Fujiwara mother ascended the throne and promptly set about to reassert its prerogatives. Since the emperorship had by this time become overburdened with ritual demands, the new emperor, Gosanjō, relinquished it with the apparent aim of exercising greater administrative powers as a retired or cloistered emperor. Gosanjō died within a year of his abdication; but his son, Shirakawa, inaugurated a system of cloistered emperors who rivalled the Fujiwara at court during the next century and even retained a certain political pre-eminence in Kyoto after the rise of the military in the late 1100s.

The cloistered emperors of the late eleventh and early twelfth centuries sought to secure the support of men from families other than the Fujiwara. At first they turned to the Minamoto, but later they gave special preference to the Taira. As the Taira gained influence at court, they also acquired important estate holdings throughout the western provinces. They thus placed themselves geographically in opposition to the Minamoto of the east. Within decades these two great samurai clans were to contend for control of the entire country.

2
Rise of the Samurai

The twelfth century was a time of momentous upheaval in Japan. The Heian courtiers had for centuries failed to provide proper administration in the provinces and had allowed control everywhere to pass into the hands of local magnates, who had taken up arms and formed a professional warrior class. By the middle of the twelfth century the courtiers had shown themselves unable to manage even their own personal affairs in the capital. The halcyon days when the noble had nothing more to concern himself with than the turning of an apt couplet or the pursuit of a romantic whim were over. Armed warriors of the Taira and Minamoto clans could be seen everywhere in the streets of Kyoto and, with quarrels between the feuding factions of both courtiers and samurai occurring more and more frequently, the populace had become anxious and apprehensive.

When the cloistered emperor Toba, who had been the undisputed patriarch of the imperial family, died suddenly in 1156, violence finally erupted in a dispute between two of his sons, the former emperor Sutoku and the reigning sovereign, Goshirakawa. Rival members of the Fujiwara clan, as well as samurai of the Taira and Minamoto houses, lined up behind both Sutoku and Goshirakawa and sought to use this royal dispute as an opportunity to settle their own diverse grievances. The brief but bloody encounter that ensued is known after the year-period as the Hōgen Incident.

The Hōgen Incident caused the grim spectacle of brother warring against brother and father against son. Although the conflict was actually decided in a single battle fought at night, it was of great historical significance in bringing about a decisive shift of national leadership from the courtiers of Kyoto to the provincial military. The latter were still sharply divided among

themselves and had not even acted as unified families in the
fighting of Hōgen. Yet the period of courtier dominance of Japan
was clearly over and that of the samurai had begun. The samurai
could no longer be used as mercenaries by the Heian nobles, but
would henceforth act directly in their own interests.

One of the foremost of Sutoku's supporters in the Hōgen
Incident was Fujiwara Yorinaga, a severe Confucian moralist
who thought only in terms of courtier supremacy and who had no
real understanding of the significance of the rise of the samurai
class. Yorinaga appears in the records of the time as the very
personification of the old order of autocratic and unyielding
nobles who were losing out so rapidly to the vigorous new
warriors from the provinces. Nowhere can Yorinaga's ignorance
of the samurai class be seen more strikingly than in an incident
which occurred just before the Hōgen hostilities when Sutoku's
followers gathered in one of the palaces of Kyoto to discuss
their strategy. Among the Minamoto allied to Sutoku was a
youth named Tametomo, who possessed prodigious physical
strength and at seventeen was already a renowned fighter.
Tametomo, described by the pro-Minamoto chronicles of
the following century as 'seven feet tall' and armed with a
bow measuring eight and a half feet in length, urged that
they launch a night attack and set fire to the enemy position.
In any fighting that might ensue the only enemy chieftain that
in his opinion they need worry about was his own older brother,
Yoshitomo, and Tametomo promised to deal personally with
him.

Yorinaga replied haughtily that, although such crude tactics
might be useful in private battles among the samurai, they were
hardly appropriate to a dispute which involved the imperial
family and which could well decide the fate of the country. The
best and most fitting policy, he declared, was a defensive one:
await reinforcements from the former capital of Nara to the south,
which Yorinaga expected by the following morning.

Having been rebuked by such a lofty personage as Yorinaga,
Tametomo could do nothing but mumble as he withdrew that,
if they did not advance before dawn, his brother Yoshitomo
would surely employ the same strategy and lead the enemy

forces to attack *them*. And indeed that is precisely what happened.
Yoshitomo and his temporary Taira allies stormed the position
of the ex-emperor Sutoku's backers that night, set it ablaze and,
after a fierce struggle, routed its occupants. Tametomo defended
mightily, holding off scores of attackers single-handedly, we are

Samurai in full battle dress, from an early nineteenth-century design
for a sword-guard

told; yet in the end even his great fighting strength was not
sufficient to cancel the advantage which the enemy had seized by
attacking first at night.

   In the aftermath of the Hōgen Incident some of the most
prominent members of Sutoku's party were put to death in the

first public executions carried out in Kyoto in three and a half centuries. These provided a shocking spectacle, especially when Yoshitomo, at the insistence of the throne, beheaded his own father and the Taira chieftain, Kiyomori, killed his uncle. Yoshitomo's brother Tametomo was spared the death penalty, but was banished to a distant province after the tendons in his bow arm had been severed.

Tametomo, like his eleventh century forebear, Yoshiie, is a semi-legendary figure in the history of the samurai and has inspired a number of fabulous tales dealing with his exploits, especially after the Hōgen Incident. Despite the handicap of losing the use of his prodigiously powerful bow arm, Tametomo once again became a feared warrior chieftain and travelled widely to engage in armed struggles and in what the court regarded as lawless mischief. He is even supposed on one occasion to have journeyed as far as the Ryukyu Islands to the south of Japan, where he married the daughter of a local territorial leader and produced a son who founded a line of kings of the Ryukyus. Tametomo's end came in 1170 when, after defeat in a battle in the east, he committed *seppuka*. His disembowelment is generally regarded as the first convincingly verifiable instance of this act.

A bare three years after the Hōgen Incident, fighting broke out once again in Kyoto. This time the lines of opposition were more clearly drawn as the Taira arrayed themselves on one side and the Minamoto on the other. One of the principal causes of the struggle of Heiji, as this second incident came to be known, was Minamoto Yoshitomo's dissatisfaction over the fact that, after the Hōgen fighting, his erstwhile ally Taira Kiyomori had received greater honour and reward from the court than he. In 1159 Yoshitomo, in league with a Fujiwara minister who was also disgruntled over his failure to achieve high rank, took advantage of Kiyomori's temporary absence from the capital to execute a *coup* at court.

When Kiyomori and the Taira rushed back to Kyoto, the stage was set for a seemingly inevitable clash between the two greatest warrior clans of the land. Before the fighting began, however, the Taira succeeded in engineering the escape of the emperor, disguised as a lady-in-waiting, from the custody of the Minamoto to their own camp. This move was of crucial importance to the Taira cause even though the emperor at that time was a mere youth of seventeen and could exercise little or no real authority on his own. Contestants in major civil conflicts in Japanese history have invariably sought to legitimize their acts, even when they were really motivated by lust for power or greed for material gain, by asserting that they undertook them for the emperor. In the case of the Heiji struggle, which took place in the capital, the physical presence of the emperor in the Taira camp automatically sanctified their side as the 'rightful' one.

The Taira in this instance went on to win a great military victory, completely decimating the leadership of the Minamoto clan and establishing themselves as the new masters of Japan. Had they lost despite the psychological advantage of possession of the emperor, however, it would have been necessary for others to rationalize the loss in some fashion such as averring that the emperor had in fact been held against his will or that the Taira had not really acted in his interests. A cynical Japanese proverb states that 'those who win are the emperor's army, while those who lose are rebels'.

The Taira ruled Japan for more than twenty years. The age of their supremacy and the renewal of warfare with the Minamoto in the 1180s which brought it to a close are vividly portrayed in one of the first of the great war tales of the medieval period, the *Tale of the Heike* (an alternate name for the Taira). This work, which was written some fifty to seventy-five years after the events with which it deals, depicts the Taira as haughty upstarts who, after a period of ascendancy, were doomed to ultimate destruction and oblivion. Because of the darkly fatalistic tone of this famous war tale, which gained popularity through the ages as much from having its episodes chanted by itinerant storytellers as being read as a work of literature, the history of the Taira has traditionally been viewed as one of predestined tragedy. The sense of tragedy surrounding the Taira was further deepened by the widespread mood of pessimism that accompanied the military upheavals of the twelfth century. Although the samurai class was to provide Japan with far more vigorous and effective rule than the Heian courtiers ever had, people of that epoch viewed the rise of the military to power as a sure sign that society and its values had sadly declined.

Kiyomori, the dictator who dominated the period of Taira hegemony, was a man of highly changeable temperament: stubborn and blustering at one moment, gentle and even charming the next. Such mercurial behaviour was apparently a common characteristic during this swashbuckling age, although Kiyomori seems to have been more extreme than most. The *Tale of the Heike* and other records draw a sharp contrast between him and his son Shigemori, whom they credit with keeping the irresolute elder Taira in check, and with being the real architect of the family's successes. Kiyomori's supposed ineptitude under fire is amusingly recounted in a tale from the Heiji struggle. Late in the fighting when the Minamoto sought to attack the Taira position in a futile effort to recoup their earlier reverses, Kiyomori, excited and apparently flustered by the thought of impending combat, put his armour on backward. When this was pointed out to him, he blithely retorted that, since the emperor was in the building which they would have to defend, he had deliberately reversed his armour in order not to offend his majesty by having the front of it turned to him while he, Kiyomori, fought.

On another occasion some years later Kiyomori again donned his armour to ride against the cloistered emperor Goshirakawa, who had been privy to a plot to overthrow the Taira. Shigemori deplored this impetuous action and set out to the main Taira mansion to reprimand his father. When Kiyomori learned of his son's approach he quickly donned a robe. But much to his embarrassment it kept slipping open to reveal the bulky pieces of his battle attire beneath.

The untimely death in 1178 of Shigemori, pictured always as the wise counsellor of the Taira, was a great blow to the future prospects of the clan.

After Shigemori's death the popularity of the Taira declined abysmally. In their arrogance and willfulness this self-styled warrior-courtier family had managed to anger and alienate people in all segments of Kyoto society. So widespread was the enmity towards them that before long members of the rival Minamoto

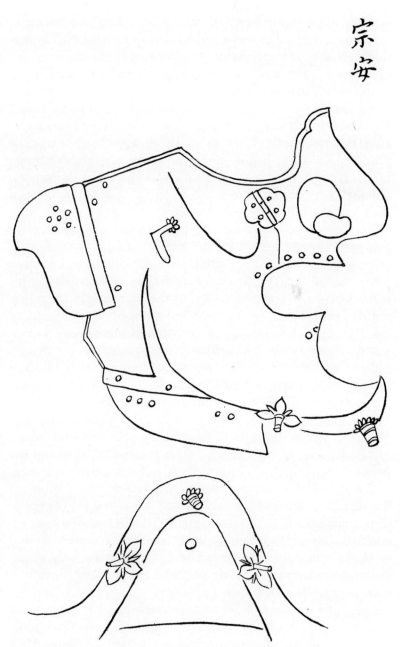

宗安

Face-mask from *Illustrated Survey of Famous Armour* by Shokwanzan

clan scattered throughout the eastern provinces and elsewhere became encouraged to seek a revival of their own national aspirations. Among the earliest of the Minamoto chieftains to rise against the Taira was Yoritomo, who took up arms in the east in the eighth month of 1180.

Yoritomo was one of several sons of Yoshitomo whom Kiyomori, to his later agonizing regret, had allowed to survive after the Heiji struggle of 1159. In an apparently incredible blunder, Kiyomori had even permitted the youthful Yoritomo to be exiled to the eastern provinces where the Minamoto, although temporarily beaten and dispirited, had always enjoyed their greatest following and support.

Yoritomo, after defeating the Taira armies sent eastward to deal with him as a 'rebel', did not seek immediately to mount an offensive against the Taira position in the central and western provinces. Instead, he devoted his energies to consolidating his control over the east and to laying the foundations for a new military government in the small but strategically well-situated fishing village of Kamakura to the south of present-day Tokyo. His decision to make his permanent headquarters in the eastern rather than the central provinces was to have a crucial influence on the future course of Japanese history. The Kantō Plain is ten times more wealthy in agricultural land than any other part of Japan, and, once under the mastery of a great leader like Yoritomo, it was shown to be the best possible base from which to rule the rest of the country. With the rise of Yoritomo the political centre of gravity of Japan was shifted decisively eastward.

While Yoritomo concentrated on strengthening his position in the east, he more and more entrusted the actual field generalship against the Taira to his brilliant half-brother, Yoshitsune, who was destined to become one of the most celebrated samurai in Japanese history. The legend of Yoshitsune has been retold and embellished so frequently that we have difficulty discerning with any clarity what he was really like.

Very little is known of Yoshitsune's early life. His mother was a court beauty, wooed by Minamoto Yoshitomo, who gave birth to Yoshitsune just a few months before the Heiji Incident. After the crushing Minamoto defeat in this conflict, the mother is purported to have become Kiyomori's concubine and the child himself to have been placed in a monastery. Upon reaching the age of awareness, however, Yoshitsune showed a strong dislike for the priesthood and managed to escape to the northern provinces where he grew to adulthood under the patronage of a provincial branch of the Fujiwara and became a devout student of the military arts.

Later generations have embroidered a great variety of miraculous tales about Yoshitsune's youth. Although of slight build

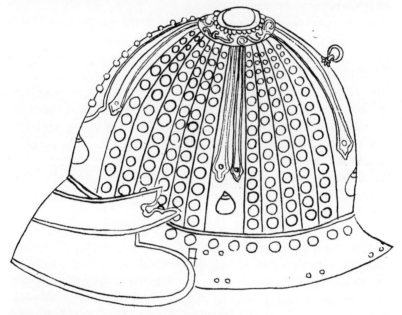

Helmet from *Illustrated Survey of Famous Armour*

(with bulging eyes and crooked teeth, one regrets to note), he is said to have become a superb, almost superhuman, swordsman, and a leader of magnetic personality. Gradually he, like Robin Hood, gathered about him a band of loyal and gallant fighters, the most noted of whom was the burly monk Benkei, the Little John of Japanese history. Benkei is described in the legendary accounts as a huge brute of a man who enjoyed nothing so much as a good brawl. He is supposed at one time to have taken a vow to confiscate a thousand swords from lone and unsuspecting men

whom he trapped night after night in the streets of the capital.
After collecting 999 swords, he went out cheerfully in search of
the last. Shortly before dawn Benkei's opportunity came.When
it did, however, it hardly seemed a worthy way to finish such a
great project, for the would-be victim approaching him was a
mere lad playing plaintively on his flute. The lad, of course, was
none other than Yoshitsune, who not only refused to relinquish
his weapon but treated Benkei to such a dazzling display of
swordsmanship that before long the latter had capitulated and
had vowed to serve Yoshitsune for life.

Quite apart from this and other fanciful legends, there seems
to be little doubt that Yoshitsune was in fact one of the greatest
military geniuses in the annals of Japan. In 1184 and 1185 he
defeated the Taira in a series of spectacular campaigns, ranging
from the shores of the Inland Sea south of the capital to Dannoura
at the western end of Honshu. Yoshitsune's tactics were distinguished by qualities that were to herald a new age in Japanese
warfare: bold and imaginative planning, lightning-like surprise
attacks and an ability to beat the enemy at his own game, as in
the climactic battle of Dannoura in 1185 when Yoshitsune took
to the sea to destroy the fleet of the Taira, who had long been
noted for their naval power.

At the battle of Ichinotani in 1184, when the Taira were en-
camped on a beach of the Inland Sea with a steep and rugged
slope protecting them in the rear, Yoshitsune sent the main
Minamoto force to attack from the front by sea. After waiting
until the armies were engaged in fierce combat, he came roaring
down a defile with a hand-picked group of riders to rout the
enemy from behind and set their fortifications ablaze. In utter
confusion, the Taira and their adherents scattered and sought to
escape either on horseback or by sea.

Kumagai Naozane, a captain of the Minamoto side, spied one
of the enemy attempting to board a ship from the beach. Judged
from his magnificent armour, he was a Taira general of high
rank. Yet when Kumagai wrestled him to the ground and tore
off his helmet, he was astonished to find himself gazing upon the
countenance of a lovely youth of sixteen or seventeen made up in
the courtly manner with powdered skin and blackened teeth.

above : Members of the Taira clan respectfully bow to the emperor (hidden in the ox-drawn carriage) after his dramatic escape at the time of the Heiji Incident in 1159.

below : The Taira triumphantly escorting the emperor to their camp.

The Sanjō Palace in Kyoto is fired during the
cruel and chaotic Heiji Incident.

above : Yoshitsune and Benkei fight on a bridge in Kyoto : Yoshitsune gives a dazzling display of swordsmanship.

Yoshitsune as portrayed
by the nineteenth-century
artist, Kuniyoshi.

Yoshitsune gallantly
leads his forces into battle
(nineteenth-century print).

above : The youthful Atsumori, who has desperately attempted to board a ship at the beach, looks back at his fierce assailant (Kumagai); in his belt Atsumori carries his famous flute.

right : Kumagai eagerly pursues his prey during the battle of Ichinotani (1184).

Scenes from the civil wars between the Taira
and the Minamoto.

Kumagai, who had a son the same age, would have released his prisoner forthwith but glancing up he saw several of his own Minamoto allies riding hard towards them and knew there was no hope for escape. Tearfully he explained to the youth, whose name he later learned to be Atsumori, the outrages to which he might be subjected if taken alive and, upon receiving Atsumori's understanding approval, struck off his head. Later, in removing the youth's armour, Kumagai discovered a small pouch at his waist containing a flute. He recalled with almost unbearable sadness that he had heard the notes of such an instrument, probably the same, drifting gently across the space separating the rival encampments the night before the battle of Ichinotani.

The story of Kumagai and Atsumori is one of the best loved in Japanese literature. According to the *Tale of the Heike*, this grievous experience caused Kumagai to turn his back on the world and to enter the Buddhist priesthood in order to devote the rest of his life to prayer for Atsumori's soul. In point of fact, other sources reveal that Kumagai did nothing of the sort. He was apparently in actual life a very quarrelsome, litigious man. He did eventually take Buddhist vows some eight years after his chance meeting with Atsumori but his reason then was a fit of pique over the loss of a dispute at law with another samurai concerning a holding of land.

When Yoshitsune emerged victorious over the Taira at the sea battle of Dannoura, he returned to Kyoto a great national hero. Yet the seemingly richly deserved honours that he received from the court at this time served only to heighten the suspicion of his half-brother and commander, Yoritomo, in Kamakura. One reason why Yoritomo had founded his military government in the east had been to avoid as much as possible the social mingling of court nobles and warriors, which, he was convinced, would only soften and spoil the latter. He believed, moreover, that his vassals should be beholden to him alone and should under no circumstances accept rewards from outside sources without his express approval. If the celebrated Yoshitsune could receive honours from the imperial court without reference to him, surely others among the Minamoto and their followers would soon come to view this as an entirely appropriate thing to do.

4

Once his heart was set against Yoshitsune, Yoritomo showed him little mercy. No doubt there was reason for his suspicion that the open and impulsive Yoshitsune, although a brilliant field general, lacked the qualities necessary for peace-time leadership. Yet there was also a personal streak of cruel perversity in Yoritomo which he seemed to direct with the greatest vigour against members of his own family.

When, in the fifth month of 1185, Yoshitsune travelled to Kamakura for his first meeting with his brother since Dannoura, Yoritomo curtly refused him entry to the city. Although Yoshitsune sent an emotional and pathetically worded letter imploring Yoritomo to remember their bond of kinship and to reconsider his decision, it appears to have had no discernable effect and Yoshitsune was finally obliged to return disconsolately to Kyoto. Shortly thereafter he set out to the west with a small band of followers in the desperate hope of establishing his own base of power in the provinces.

It is with the tragic final years of his wandering, first in the western and then in the northern provinces, that the extensive literature on Yoshitsune is most concerned. Interestingly, as the tales of wandering progress, Yoshitsune becomes more and more a forlorn and even effeminate figure and real leadership of his band of followers reverts to the ever-faithful henchman, Benkei. One of the great moments in the Kabuki theatre takes place in a scene from the play entitled *Kanjinchō* ('The Subscription List') in which Benkei attempts to lead Yoshitsune and the rest of the band, disguised as monks, through a mountain pass guarded by men put on special alert by Yoritomo. Benkei, with some glib talking, gets them nearly safely through the pass when the captain of the guards suddenly stops Yoshitsune, who is laggardly bringing up the rear. Quickly interceding, Benkei curses and even strikes the slight figure of Yoshitsune in order to demonstrate that he is a mere underling who deserves no special attention from the captain. There have been few dry eyes among Japanese audiences through the ages as they have shared with Benkei the anguish and agony he feels when he is thus forced to turn upon his beloved master in order to save him from fatal detection. In Benkei the Japanese have seen one of the finest flowerings of the spirit of unswerving devotion that was, at least in literature, the most redeeming feature of the medieval samurai.

During the epic events that accompanied the rise of the samurai in the late twelfth century, heroism was not restricted to men. There is, for example, a poignant tale concerning Yoshi-tsune's mistress, Shizuka, who started out with her lover on his wanderings to the west but was forced to return to the capital when she could no longer keep up with the rigours of hard travelling. Shizuka, who was at the time regarded as a great beauty and by many as the finest singer and dancer in all Japan, was subsequently captured and transported to Kamakura, where she was forced to perform before Yoritomo. Defiantly Shizuka sang a song that expressed her undying love and yearning for Yoshitsune. Yoritomo was outraged and might have inflicted severe punishment upon her had not his wife, who was also an exceptionally strong-willed person, interceded.

Tales of devotion and sacrifice by women for their menfolk are common enough during the medieval period, yet one reads very little about reciprocity on the part of men. There is, indeed, nothing in the samurai tradition that compares to the idealiza-tion of feminine virtue and love that was so important a motivat-ing factor for chivalric behaviour in Europe's high Middle Ages. The Japanese warrior simply did not enter battle with the thought of performing great deeds for a mistress or for some un-attainable paragon of womanhood. Although the medieval period in Japan may in some respects have been 'epic', it never became 'romantic'.

Yoshitsune's end was pathetic in a peculiarly Japanese way. The Japanese sentiment has always been especially touched by the thought of the great hero perishing alone, or nearly so, in a remote region. After various adventures about which we know more from literature than history, Yoshitsune and his small band finally arrived in the northern provinces where they sought the protection of the Fujiwara chieftain who had been Yoshitsune's childhood patron. For a while things went well, but when the old chieftain died one of his sons treacherously decided to destroy Yoshitsune in order to ingratiate himself with Yoritomo. According to the *Gikeiki*, a fifteenth-century work which is the

best single source for the legends of Yoshitsune, Benkei and some
nine other retainers fought against no less than thirty thousand
troops who attacked Yoshitsune's residence in a bravura scene
that could scarcely be topped by even the most imaginative of
Japan's screenwriters today.

While the others fought, Yoshitsune sat in the back of the
house calmly reciting the Buddhist *Lotus Sutra*. Before long
Benkei rushed in to inform his master that only Kataoka and he
of the band of retainers still remained alive and that Kataoka was
at that time holding off the attackers out front. Yoshitsune asked
Benkei to allow him a little more time to finish his recitation
and then to kill his wife, his children and himself. After returning
once more to exchange poems with Yoshitsune about their meeting in the Buddhist paradise of the next world, Benkei rejoined
Kataoka in the struggle against the thirty thousand. Even after
Kataoka died, Benkei fought on alone, rushing into the enemy
lines time and again. Although innumerable arrows lodged in
his armour, he simply bent them down and paid them no further
heed. At length he stood in the midst of the enemy, a great giant
of a man whom nobody dared approach. Yet when finally someone rode near, the wind from his horse caught Benkei and down
he sprawled. It was only then that the attackers realized he had
already been dead on his feet for several minutes.

3
Repelling the Mongols

Yoritomo's military government is known as the Kamakura Shogunate from the title of *shōgun* or 'generalissimo' which he received from the Kyoto court in 1192. Shoguns of the eighth and ninth centuries had been great courtier-generals who had conducted campaigns against the aboriginal Emishi tribesmen in the regions of the east and north where Yoritomo now held his military hegemony. Although he had achieved this hegemony by his own efforts alone, Yoritomo was meticulously careful to maintain the outward appearance of absolute loyalty to the throne. As shogun, or the emperor's first commander for military affairs, he could justify his founding of a separate warrior administration as a necessary step for maintaining order in the land. Yoritomo was able, moreover, to extend his authority outward from the east through the appointment of his vassals or shogunal housemen as 'stewards' and 'constables' to various estates and provinces of the country.

Yoritomo, who was otherwise one of the greatest leaders in Japanese history, erred grievously only in his failure to provide for a smooth succession to the office of shogun. Owing apparently to a pathological suspicious nature, he destroyed not only Yoshitsune but also several other of his most prominent kinsmen and thus seriously weakened the ranks of the Minamoto clan. There was no immediate danger to Minamoto leadership so long as Yoritomo himself remained alive, since none of his vassal barons dared challenge him. But when Yoritomo died suddenly in 1199 his two sons – who became in turn the second and third Minamoto shoguns – were helpless to keep these barons in check. By the end of the second decade of the thirteenth century both had been killed and power in the shogunate was seized by the family of Hōjō.

The patriarch of the Hōjō family, Tokimasa, had been one of two men appointed to watch over Yoritomo during the latter's exile in the east after the Heiji Incident of 1159. Tokimasa did more than 'watch over' Yoritomo; he became an intimate associate of his and one of the first to urge the Minamoto chieftain to rise against the Taira in 1180. Yoritomo further cemented

Minamoto Yoritomo

relations between the Minamoto and the Hōjō by marrying Tokimasa's daughter, the bold and forceful Masako, who interceded on behalf of Shizuka when she sang of her love for Yoshitsune.

It was characteristically Japanese that the Hōjō, once they had emerged supreme in the power struggle following Yoritomo's death, did not seek to become shoguns themselves. Instead, they assumed ruling authority at Kamakura through the office of shogunal regent, which they opened. Such was the importance attached to aristocratic and hierarchic qualifications in pre-modern Japan that both court nobles and warrior chieftains were highly reluctant, if not completely unwilling, to assume positions to which they were not clearly entitled by birth. The Hōjō – who were of modest, even obscure – origins, were quite content to allow others (first members of the Fujiwara family and later imperial princes) to act as figurehead shoguns while they held real power in the hierarchically inferior post of shogunal regent.

The Hōjō provided pre-modern Japan with some of its best government during their tenure as regents from 1219 until 1333. They established a Council of State, by which they permitted other leading shogunal housemen to have a voice in shogunate affairs, and they compiled a new legal code for military society that enabled them and the council to adjudicate disputes over land and other matters with surprising justice. In 1221 a cloistered emperor in Kyoto attempted to overthrow the Kamakura Shogunate, but his abortive effort only provided the Hōjō with the opportunity to impress shogunal rule more firmly than before upon the imperial court. For most of the remainder of the Kamakura period the Hōjō regents held the court in a state of political impotence, even going so far as to dictate succession to the throne.

A great threat to Hōjō rule and to Japan arose in the 1270s from the Mongol Dynasty of China. While the Minamoto and the Hōjō had been busy building Japan's first warrior government, momentous events had been happening on the continent. About the turn of the thirteenth century the greatest military power the world had yet seen was forged and set in motion in central Asia by the renowned Mongol leader, Genghis Khan. Within a few decades Mongol hordes had swept over most of Asia and had even penetrated into regions of Eastern Europe, such as Poland, Hungary and Bohemia. The Mongols were horse-riding nomads who could live in the saddle for days on end and were capable of travelling great distances in brief periods of time. With their complex cavalry tactics, their speed and striking power, they were virtually irresistible to most of the peoples they encountered in their drive to dominate the Eurasian continent.

Although the Mongols did not actually subjugate the south of China until 1279, they established their rule over north China at a much earlier date and, under Genghis's gifted grandson, Khubilai Khan, founded the Yuan or 'Original' Dynasty in 1270. It was Khubilai Khan who first sent messengers to Japan imperiously demanding that the Japanese acknowledge China's suzerainty over east Asia and forthwith submit tribute to the Mongol court.

China, the great 'Middle Kingdom' of East Asia, had traditionally attempted to force its smaller, neighbouring states to accept a subservient, 'tributary' relationship towards it. Such a relationship obliged them periodically to send tribute missions to China and to pay homage at the Chinese court. One advantage of the missions to the smaller states was that Imperial China almost invariably bestowed greater gifts upon them than they brought as tribute to it. Nevertheless, the tributary relationship was distinctly one of inferiority *vis-à-vis* China; and Japan, alone among the countries of east Asia, had for centuries steadfastly refused to conform to it.

When Khubilai's first message arrived in Japan, the Kyoto court was at a loss how to proceed. The Hōjō regent, however, summarily refused to acquiesce to the demand for submission and sent the Mongol messenger back to China with a negative reply. No doubt the Japanese in their remote islands were not as well informed as the other peoples of Asia and eastern Europe about the ferocity and seeming invincibility of the Mongols. Yet, even allowing for a certain ignorance on their part, we must credit the Hōjō regent and his advisers with extraordinary courage for assuming the defiant stand they did. The Great Khan was predictably outraged and promptly began preparations to invade and conquer Japan.

The two attempted Mongol invasions of Japan will probably always remain something of a mystery to historians. They certainly were gigantic undertakings: the first one in 1274 was made by some forty thousand mixed Mongol, Chinese and

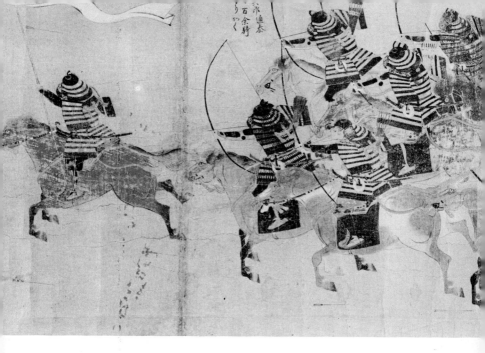

top : A group of samurai attack the Mongols in Kyushu (from the *Mongol Invasion Scroll*).

bottom : A company of sea-borne samurai press the counter-attack against the Mongols.

above : Mongol bowman.

preceding page : The samurai proudly return after defeating the Mongol forces, the most powerful army in the thirteenth-century world.

above : Takesaki Suenaga, the samurai who commissioned the
Mongol Invasion Scroll, pits his strength against the alien forces.

Three members of the loyalist Kusunoki family make their last stand on behalf of the emperor in 1348 (nineteenth-century print by Kuniyoshi).

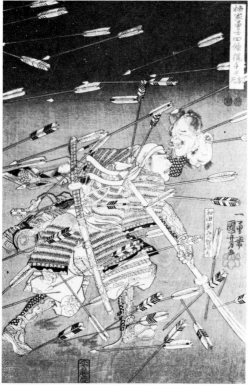

above : A squadron of *kamikaze* pilots make a final salute before flying off to certain death in World War II.

below : *Kamikaze* pilots joyfully preparing to board their planes.

Korean troops and the second one in 1281 by perhaps as many as one hundred thousand. William the Conqueror's invasion of Britain in 1066 at the head of some fifteen hundred knights and their supporting men was a puny expedition by comparison. Yet is it possible that Khubilai Khan ordered these vast and almost prohibitively expensive invasions purely from the megalomaniacal desire to bring still another people to their knees? Apparently so despite the fact that Japan could have provided the world-conquering Mongols with little more than they already possessed.

The first invasion attempt was brief. The Mongols, after overrunning several Japanese-occupied islands in the Straits of Korea, landed in the region of Hakata Bay in northern Kyushu. Although the samurai warriors of Kyushu who responded to the call to defend appear to have fought stoutly enough, they were manifestly out-classed by the invaders, who manoeuvred in closely-ordered groups and used bells, gongs and other devices to signal to each other. The Mongols also exposed the Japanese for the first time to the frightening effects of gunpowder by firing large iron 'exploding balls' at them. Yet it was not until the Portuguese introduced European firearms to Japan nearly three centuries later that the Japanese made any serious attempt to adapt gunpowder to their own military purposes. This can be at least partly explained by the generalization that feudal warriors, whether in Europe, Japan or elsewhere, are slow to adopt new methods and weapons that are likely to undermine their own positions as the possessors of traditionally accepted and specialized techniques of warfare. Whereas men in a modern society are by the fact of their modernity committed to change, the military leaders of a feudal society are by and large highly resistant to it.

After inflicting severe punishment on the Japanese defenders and on the countryside where the battle of the first invasion took place, the enemy withdrew to their ships at the end of the day. That night a great storm arose which forced the Mongols back out to sea and caused them heavy losses. By the time the armada had straggled back to the continent, some thirteen thousand men had been drowned.

The Japanese were far better prepared to resist the Mongols
5

when they reappeared seven years later in the summer of 1281 to make their second effort at invasion. In addition to manning a new coastal defence system the samurai also set forth into Hakata Bay with great intrepidity in a Drake-like fleet of small ships to harass the much larger Mongol troop vessels and temporarily to disrupt their landing plans. Although the subsequent fighting on land lasted for nearly two months, this invasion attempt, like the first, was abruptly terminated by a great storm that forced the Mongols back to their vessels and blew them out to sea. The losses they sustained this time were even more appalling than during the bad weather of 1274.

One remarkable legacy of the Mongol invasions is the Mongol Invasion Scroll, important portions of which have come down to us today. This magnificently detailed work, which was painted at the request of a Kyushu samurai named Takezaki Suenaga (who fought in both the 1274 and 1281 engagements), celebrates in pictorial form, with accompanying notations, Suenaga's meritorious service in the first invasion and the trip he took to the east during the interim years to claim and receive reward from the Kamakura Shogunate. In addition to its value as a work of art, the Mongol Scroll is a highly informative commentary on samurai attitudes and behaviour during the late thirteenth century.

There is no more convincing proof of the continuing persistance of the samurai's individualistic style of fighting – his efforts to engage in direct, man-to-man combat, his paramount concern for personal recognition and reward – than in the story of Suenaga as recounted in the Mongol Scroll. On the day of the 1274 invasion Suenaga was posted with other samurai and their followers on a beach outside Hakata. Since it appeared that the Mongol landings would not extend as far as their position, Suenaga for one became exceedingly apprehensive that they might miss the action altogether. Accordingly, he announced to the commander in charge – and this was apparently an entirely accepted procedure – that he had decided to strike out, with only his four personal followers, to the area of anticipated landing on Hakata Bay. Suenaga requested that the commander inform Kamakura if he, Suenaga, should be fortunate enough to be

among the first to engage the enemy or should otherwise
distinguish himself.

When Suenaga reached one of the Mongol landing points he
was faced immediately with a dilemma. There were a number of
the enemy just waiting to be attacked, but no other samurai
around to act as witness if he should advance. It was a very risky
business from the standpoint of later reward to engage in combat without a witness, and one of his followers told him so. But
Suenaga decided to take this risk and ordered his men to attack.
In the encounter, which is graphically depicted in the Mongol
Scroll, Suenaga and two of his followers were wounded. They
probably all would have been killed but for the extraordinarily
timely appearance of another samurai leading about a hundred
men. To Suenaga the blessing of this samurai's arrival was double,
since he could act both as his rescuer and his witness.

Suenaga had, to all appearances, acted in the very best samurai
fashion and had truly distinguished himself during the 1274
invasion. Yet for some unknown reason the shogunate official in
Kyushu who should have recommended him for reward to
Kamakura did not do so, and Suenaga felt impelled to journey
to the east to plead his case personally. He claimed two points
of distinction in the fighting against the Mongols: that he had
been first in an encounter with the enemy and that he had been
wounded. He further maintained that he had suffered a loss of
face when the Kyushu official failed to submit his name for
reward and that this also should be considered in dealing with
him. Suenaga's persistence was ultimately rewarded when in the
tenth month of 1275 he received appointment to the steward-
ship of an estate in Kyushu for his services the year before.
He was among 120 housemen or retainers similarly granted
compensation by the shogunate at this time.

Suenaga, according to the Mongol Scroll, did much praying
about this time at both Shinto shrines and Buddhist temples,
imploring various deities and Buddhas before the invasion that he
might distinguish himself in battle and, afterwards, that he
might receive a bountiful reward. Yet not once, so far as we can
tell, did he pray for the protection or survival of his country.
That is, his concern was exclusively for distinction and reward

for himself and his family and not in the least for 'Japan'. In the conditions of Japan's early feudal age the abstract concept of nationhood was apparently one that never occurred to Suenaga and his kind.

There nonetheless were stirrings of sentiments at another level during the years of the Mongol invasions that were to contribute importantly to the nationalistic attitudes of the Japanese in later centuries. The two defences against the Mongols had been carried out chiefly by the samurai of Kyushu. Yet many people appear, during this intensely religious and superstitious age, to have greatly discounted the contributions of these valiant warriors and to have attributed victory over the Mongols almost exclusively to the violent storms that arose to decimate the Mongol armadas. There came to be a strong belief that these storms were in fact 'divine winds' or *kamikaze* that had been purposely unleashed by the gods to protect Japan against foreign invaders. The popular conviction among later Japanese that in times of the gravest national peril *kamikaze* would again be visited on Japan's enemies was horrifyingly displayed to the world when suicide pilots during the Pacific War were regarded as incarnations of the 'divine winds' which were then expected to save Japan from total destruction.

The Kamakura Shogunate never fully recovered from the Mongol invasions. Many other factors may also be cited to explain the decline and fall of the shogunate in the late thirteenth and early fourteenth centuries. But the most plausible of these were in one way or another aggravated by the stress of the shogunate's having to meet two actual invasion attempts and of maintaining the defence against a possible third one until about 1300.

In the early fourteenth century the imperial court, although it had long been shorn of all governing powers, gradually came to be the rallying point for those people discontented with shogunate rule. In 1324 and again in 1331 the emperor Godaigo became involved in plots against the Hōjō – in the first instance covertly and in the second openly – which were not successful but which caused great alarm in Kamakura. After the 1331 incident the Hōjō exiled Godaigo to an island off the western coast of

Honshu and placed another member of the imperial family on the throne in his place.

The matter, however, could not be settled simply by ridding the capital of Godaigo. There were many people by this time in Kyoto and elsewhere who regarded the shogunate as a thoroughly unworthy government and who were turning increasingly to support of the 'loyalist' cause of Godaigo's backers. At length in 1333 a vast array of forces, including those of the great eastern chieftain Ashikaga Takauji, who was the head of a branch family of the Minamoto and had until recently served the Hōjō, rose up and destroyed the Kamakura regime.

Godaigo thereupon returned triumphantly to the capital, reassumed the throne and undertook a brief period of rule, known after the calendrical era as the Kemmu Restoration, in which he attempted to deal directly and personally with all matters of government. Yet his efforts to ignore the realities of warrior power and to imitate emperors of old, whom he believed to have ruled sagely and simply before the rise of the Fujiwara regents and the samurai class, were sadly impractical and anachronistic. Before long many warriors began to yearn for the return to a military form of government that would more realistically and effectively handle their needs.

In 1336 Ashikaga Takauji, who had been unable to secure the appointment of shogun from the court that he desired, turned against Godaigo's government and drove the emperor and his ministers out of Kyoto to sanctuary in the mountainous region of Yoshino to the south. From this time until 1392 there were two rival courts in Japan: the 'southern' court of Godaigo and his successors in Yoshino; and the 'northern' court in Kyoto, supported and controlled by the Ashikaga Shogunate which Takauji opened. The Ashikaga period (1336–1573), or the Muromachi period as it is also called from the situation of the new shogunate's main offices in the Muromachi section of north-eastern Kyoto, was to a great extent a time of political instability, social unrest and general warfare in Japan. Although the Ashikaga shoguns had some success during the late fourteenth and early fifteenth centuries in establishing a kind of balance of power in the central and western provinces with certain regional barons known as

daimyos, they lost their central hegemony entirely in the protracted Ōnin War of 1467–77.

The period of disunion and struggle between the northern and
southern courts, which was terminated by the Ashikaga through
extinguishment of the southern court at the end of the fourteenth century, has excited the greatest passions among later
historians and nationalists. For this was the only protracted
dynastic schism in the history of the imperial house and generations of more recent Japanese have, in extolling the unique
character of Japan's unbroken line of sovereigns from the 'time
of the gods' until the present, found it utterly impossible to
accept the thought that there could have been two 'legitimate'
courts in the fourteenth century. They have felt compelled to
judge either one or the other – the northern court or the southern
court – as having been the true seat of imperial sovereignty at
that time. During the late nineteenth and early twentieth
centuries the overwhelmingly dominant view was that it had been
the southern court, since Godaigo had never willingly relinquished his emperorship but had been forced to leave Kyoto by
Ashikaga Takauji.

Takauji, at least until the Second World War, has been viewed
as one of the vilest and most traitorous individuals in Japanese
history. Conversely, the supreme hero of the fourteenth century
civil wars and indeed the most revered samurai in the annals
of Japan is a man of almost obscure origins, who was among the
earliest to rally to Godaigo's cause, named Kusunoki Masashige.
So great a folk hero did Masashige become during the Tokugawa
period that many of the samurai activists who participated in the
final overthrow of the Tokugawa Shogunate and in the Imperial
Restoration of 1868 openly conceived of themselves as acting in
the loyalist spirit of the 'Lord Kusunoki'.

Masashige's career of greatness was a brief one, lasting only
from his first meeting with Godaigo in 1331 until his death in
battle five years later. The *Taiheiki*, the principal war tale of this
age, tells us that the coming of Masashige was supernaturally
portended to Godaigo in a dream after the emperor had fled from
the capital during the abortive 1331 attempt to overthrow the
Hōjō and the Kamakura Shogunate. Godaigo saw a great tree

before the imperial palace in Kyoto and beneath it a raised seat
facing south to which two young boys beckoned him. In both
China and Japan emperors have, on formal occasions, traditionally faced southward towards their subjects; hence, there could be
no doubt in Godaigo's mind that the raised seat of his dream
symbolized the imperial throne and that the invitation to occupy
it implied that he would soon preside over the land as its true,

Kusunoki Masashige with his son

and not simply, titular ruler. Yet beyond this apparently obvious interpretation, Godaigo also noted that, if one placed the written character for 'tree' beside that for 'south', together they comprised the Japanese word for 'camphor tree' or *kusunoki*. When he spoke to his ministers of this, they suggested that *kusunoki* might be taken to mean a warrior from a nearby province, called Kusunoki Masashige, who they had heard enjoyed an admirable reputation for the bearing of arms. Godaigo accordingly summoned Masashige and requested that he take command of the imperial forces, which at the time were none too numerous. In accepting the charge, Masashige respectfully cautioned Godaigo not to become discouraged at the news of temporary setbacks. So long as the emperor knew that he, Masashige, was still alive, he could be assured that the imperial cause would still prevail.

Although the 1331 plot against Kamakura in fact failed and Godaigo was sent into exile, Masashige and another loyalist commander, who was one of the emperor's own sons, maintained a continuous pressure on the shogunate armies through guerrilla activities in the central provinces until 1333, when the great eastern general Ashikaga Takauji and others finally joined them in overthrowing the Hōjō regime. For his contribution to the ultimate loyalist victory, Masashige was handsomely rewarded by Godaigo during the period of the Kemmu Restoration.

When Takauji at length rebelled against the throne in 1336 and made ready to attack the capital after gathering troops in the west, Masashige outspokenly opposed any all-out effort to check the Ashikaga armies as they advanced by land and water along the coast of the Inland Sea. He proposed, instead, that the loyalists temporarily relinquish Kyoto and wait until they were stronger to seek its recapture. The emperor, however, refused to heed this advice and ordered that a stand be made at Minatogawa near present-day Kobe, as suggested by another commander.

According to the *Taiheiki*, Masashige resignedly accepted the emperor's decision and entered the battle of Minatogawa in the fifth month of 1336 with the conviction that he would not survive it. At the time of his departure for the battle, he told his young son Masatsura – in words that were to ring in the ears of later generations of samurai nationalists – that, although he was prepared to forfeit his life for the throne, he wished to die knowing that Masatsura would some day take up the struggle for the imperial cause in his stead.

After his death at Minatogawa, where he fought stoutly for many hours in a hot sun before committing *seppuku*, Masashige was purportedly buried in a nearby plot. Centuries later this site was transformed into one of Japan's most hallowed shrines, especially for samurai pilgrims of the late Tokugawa period who wished to pay humble veneration to the exemplary conduct and matchless fighting spirit of 'Kusunoki, a loyal subject'.

In the Japanese tradition Kusunoki Masashige represents the greatest embodiment of imperial loyalism. The type of devotion to the throne that he is believed to have held in the highest degree was very different from the bond of feudal loyalty between samurai vassal and lord that had evolved in Japan from at least the eleventh century. Feudal loyalty was a reciprocal social relationship, entered into by two fighting-men, which was born of necessity and which was in practice usually carefully qualified as to the kind and extent of performance expected of both parties. Imperial loyalism, on the other hand, was a transcendent commitment to the Japanese throne and to its occupant as the rightful sovereign of the land. In the late Tokugawa and early modern periods it was used to overcome diverse feudal ties and to produce Japanese nationalism. Thus the evolution of imperial loyalism during the fourteenth century, especially in the behaviour of Masashige as he comes down to us in the *Taiheiki*, was of the greatest importance to the eventual making of modern Japan.

This does not mean that all Japanese of the fourteenth century, or even very many of them, burned with a sense of imperial loyalism. The evidence suggests, on the contrary, that the mentality of most samurai of this age was thoroughly 'feudal'; that is, they were concerned chiefly with the welfare of their own families and with the ties they maintained with their fighting companions. At the same time treachery and the shifting of allegiance were so common during the war between the courts that one questions whether loyalty of any kind existed among these early medieval samurai.

4
The age of provincial wars

The tenuous balance of power which the Ashikaga Shogunate held with its regional barons or daimyos from the end of the fourteenth century was decisively destroyed in the great Ōnin War of 1467–77. The origins of this, perhaps the most sanguinary conflict in medieval Japanese history, are complex; yet essentially the war arose from the inability of the various daimyos to maintain control over their domains, many of which spanned two or more provinces, and over the unruly and avaricious vassals who served in them as their deputies and administrators. By the mid-fifteenth century a number of the most important daimyo families had become embroiled in succession disputes, which provided the opportunity for vassals to take up sides and to engage in their own personal struggles for land and power. Finally, in the 1460s, the shogunal house itself fell victim to a dispute over succession.

The ruling shogun of this period, Ashikaga Yoshimasa, was of little help in dealing with the problems that beset the shogunate and the daimyos on the eve of the Ōnin War. He had grown up almost exclusively in the company of women and sychophantic attendants. Although a sumptuous entertainer and a grand patron of the arts, he appears from the records to have had little if any interest in martial affairs. Yoshimasa seems indeed to have been quite content to leave all matters of fighting, the principal occupation of the Japanese aristocracy of this age, to others. His succession to the venerable and honoured title of *sei-i tai-shōgun*, or 'barbarian-subduing generalissimo', was in itself testimony of the forfeiture by the Ashikaga of their former leadership of samurai society. Under Yoshimasa the shogunate became nearly as powerless as the imperial court and was only with difficulty propped up by certain leading daimyos who apparently still felt that it might be of use to them in pursuing their own ambitions.

Yoshimasa eventually decided that he wished nothing so much as to be rid of all political responsibilities, limited as they had become for him, in order to devote his time exclusively to cultural pursuits. Since he had no son of his own, he persuaded his brother to assume the office of shogun in his place. Yet no sooner had Yoshimasa done this than his wife gave birth to a boy and insisted that the latter be made the new shogun. In the dispute that now arose over succession to the shogunate, the samurai chieftains began to form into two great hostile camps behind the brother and the son. Yoshimasa attempted to check the momentous confrontation that impended as daimyos called their troops up to the capital from the provinces and as they began to erect defence works around their headquarters in the city. But his feeble efforts, which consisted chiefly of threatening to brand as rebels those who started fighting first, had little effect and in the fifth month of 1467 the great war of Ōnin erupted.

Much of the Ōnin War was fought within the confines of Kyoto. Although the most ferocious encounters occurred during its first years, the dreary struggle dragged on for more than a decade. When the last armies finally withdrew in 1477, they left the city in almost total ruin. The *Chronicle of Ōnin*, a war tale which is arranged in the form of a contemporary narrative but was actually written much later, records in anguished phrases that: 'The flowery capital which was expected to last for thousands of years has now become the lair of foxes and wolves . . . Although there have been disorders and vicissitudes since ancient times, in this conflict of Ōnin even the Buddhist and imperial laws have been destroyed.'

Despite the ghastly human carnage and vast material losses suffered during the protracted battling of the Ōnin War, there were no clear-cut victors. On the contrary, most of the daimyos who fought themselves to exhaustion and stalemate in the capital returned to the provinces to find their domains either hopelessly mired in local strife or irretrievably divided among their vassals.

The Japanese, borrowing the historical designation for the long epoch of conflict and struggle which preceded China's first great unification under the Ch'in Dynasty in 221 BC, call the century of their country's disunity following the Ōnin War the Period of Warring States. Despite certain possible, although remote, historical parallels with ancient China, Japan's post-Ōnin period is probably more appropriately labelled the Age of Provincial Wars, since there were few clearly defined 'states' anywhere in the land until at least the early decades of the sixteenth century.

Central governmental control was shattered in the aftermath of the Ōnin War. Although the Ashikaga Shogunate continued until 1573, it was able to exert little authority beyond a restricted range of territory in the central provinces; and the imperial court, which had been bereft of political significance for generations, fell into a state of near destitution. The coronation of the Emperor Gokashiwabara, who acceded to the throne in 1500, had to be postponed for twenty-one years because of a lack of funds; and legend has it that another emperor even descended to the practice of selling his signature in order to obtain cash. Without question this was the blackest age in the long history of Japan's imperial family.

A term that appears often in descriptions of conditions during the century of political fragmentation and veritable anarchy after the Ōnin War is *gekokujō*, or 'those below overthrow those above'. This term, which connotes widespread social upheaval and rapidly changing economic fortunes, is perhaps most readily applicable to the dramatic spectacle of daimyos seizing the power of the shogunate and of deputies rising against their feudal overlords. But the *gekokujō* spirit of the times was manifested also in frequent peasant uprisings and other disorders at the lower levels of society. Court nobles and Buddhist priests, who were still the principal writers of diaries and other records, spoke of *gekokujō* with great gloom and pessimism, sentiments which we can well understand when expressed by members of a former ruling élite whose fortunes were already in decline and who now faced further and even more sweeping change.

In contrast to the typically heroic descriptions of military actions in earlier Japanese history, eye-witness accounts of the Ōnin War more often than not stress the brutish and wantonly destructive nature of the fighting that took place in Kyoto at this time. It has been mentioned that the formalized and 'ethical' samurai combat of Minamoto Yoshiie's heyday in the late eleventh century had, during the Taira-Minamoto encounters a hundred years later, been supplemented by newer tactics of warfare aimed at taking advantage of terrain, numbers, surprise tactics and the like. Yet the Taira and Minamoto gladiators of the twelfth century had still been widely regarded as honourable and gallant warriors. Even during the struggle between the courts in the fourteenth century, when certain chieftains conspicuously violated the most basic proprieties of the unwritten samurai code and betrayal became commonplace in conduct, warfare, at least in the eyes of its contemporary chroniclers, was still considered essentially a pursuit of the lofty in spirit.

Observers of the Ōnin War, on the other hand, viewed with chilled horror and revulsion the evolution of fighting in their own day which brought to the fore a new type of combatant known as the *ashigaru* or 'lightfoot'. The *ashigaru*, who were chiefly recruited from the ranks of the peasantry, were forerunners of the ubiquitous foot-soldiers of Japanese armies of the sixteenth century. Yet whereas the latter foot-soldiers were subjected to careful military discipline by their samurai commanders, the *ashigaru* of Ōnin times were apparently scarcely controlled at all and engaged in the most wild kind of pillaging, looting, rapine and arson. To their shocked contemporaries, these vicious marauders appeared as a threat to the very future of civilized life in Japan.

Western writers of the late nineteenth century were inclined to regard most of the Ashikaga period of Japanese history as a time noteworthy only for the abysmal decline of central government, for certain cultural advances and for the accidental arrival of Europeans. They saw the age as essentially peopled by a succession of mediocrities, turncoats, sadists and perhaps worse. Although this view and its implications are generally ignored by scholars today, who prefer to probe beneath the surface of central political failure in their attempts to uncover what they regard as the more fundamental processes of historical change and development, it is quite understandable how the nineteenth century Western writers came to see at least the latter half of the Ashikaga epoch as they did.

The meaning and purpose of Japanese history, if one can talk of such things, seemed to have been lost. The Kamakura age had national order under a new military regime; and the fourteenth century had an imperial restoration and a loyalist movement in support of the southern court. But from the early fifteenth century on, the prevailing condition in Japan was disorder; and there were no great movements or causes. As the age became increasingly wretched, men themselves appear to have become more and more abominable in their behaviour. One at any rate gets this impression from reading the war tales. Earlier fighting narratives had generally pictured their protagonists as being motivated by at least some, if not necessarily a great many, of life's higher sentiments and aspirations; the main samurai combatants who appear in tales from around the time of the Ōnin War are by and large brutes.

Yet, whatever their personal qualities in our eyes, these late Muromachi samurai spawned from their midst a new and vigorous class of provincial daimyos who within a century were to make possible the founding of the most effective governing order in Japan's pre-modern history. Unlike the daimyos before the Ōnin War who had attempted to administer from above territorial spheres that were excessively large and unwieldy, these new daimyos for the most part acquired their domains gradually through force of arms and utilized every means at their disposal to maintain them as virtually independent 'states'. Among other things, they carried out cadastral surveys, encouraged the reclamation of land and the production of greater agricultural yields, sought to make conditions favourable for commercial growth (under their strict control) and undertook public works to improve domain transportation and communication.

The daimyos also compiled legal codes, or warrior 'house' laws, to dictate the behaviour of people in their realms. Some of these codes of the fifteenth and sixteenth centuries are quite detailed, prescribing such matters as military responsibilities,

social relationships, the sale and transfer of land and other
property, and commercial activities. Their essential intent was
not to grant or protect personal rights but to assess duties and to
spell out the kinds of behaviour necessary from the various
classes in order to maintain domain harmony and to facilitate the
daimyos' rule. Violaters of the codes were in almost every instance
promised harsh and speedy punishment.

Yet most of the codes tended at the same time to stress, to a
surprising degree for pre-modern times, the importance of im-
partial criteria for justice, at least for all but the daimyos and
their most privileged retainers who remained in a generally
autocratic position beyond the reach of the law. We also find the
daimyos setting down in their codes quite rational and common-
sense rules for such things as selecting men more on the basis of
merit and achievement than birth, and using the money it would
take to buy one famous sword for oneself to purchase instead a
hundred spears for one's subordinates.

An interesting entry in the code of the Asakura family directs
its vassals not to do their fighting only on 'auspicious days' nor to
plan their tactics on the basis of directional omens or taboos.
No matter how good the day or direction, it states, there is little
to be gained by heading a ship into a gale or by proceeding alone
against a vast enemy host. Yet the Asakura may have been an
exception in their efforts to debunk superstitious practices, for
the records show that other daimyo families of this age paid
careful heed to their diviners and similar practitioners of murky
lore.

One of the most significant developments during the century
of conflict following the Ōnin War was the formation by daimyos
of ever more powerful and concentrated fighting establishments.
The daimyos built central fortifications that eventually became
known as castle towns, and obliged their samurai vassals to take
up residence in them in order to be in perpetual readiness for the
call to arms; they set up hierarchical chains of command and they
increasingly enlisted the peasantry to provide infantry adjuncts
to their armies. By concentrating their efforts so intensely on
strengthening their domains in this fashion, however, the
daimyos invariably set in motion processes of militarization that

could not be checked or halted simply upon the achievement of
effective domainal security. The attitudes and aspirations of their
followers became so unalterably geared to offensive warfare that
the daimyos had little choice but to try to satisfy them through
policies of incessant aggressive campaigning against neighbouring domains.

As fighting became more and more complex in the Provincial
Wars period the daimyos also came increasingly to engage and to
rely upon specialists in the arts of military strategy and tactics.
Such specialists were known as *gunpaisha*, or 'possessors of
gunpai', large fan-like objects made of metal which these men
carried into battle and upon which they often inscribed statis-
tical information – time schedules, hours for the changing of the
tide and so on – that might be useful to them during the course
of fighting. In such demand were the truly first-rate military
specialists of this age that on one occasion in the late fifteenth
century a certain daimyo of the Kantō, after treacherously
murdering one of his vassal chiefs, promptly sought to engage
the latter's *gunpaisha* as his director of military activities despite
widespread expressions of displeasure both from his immediate
followers and from the other retainers of the dead men.

The *gunpaisha* were expected, among other things, to be
thoroughly versed in the so-called 'seven classics of warfare',
ancient military texts imported from China that were especially
popular among the samurai of medieval times. James Murdoch,
the author of a robust and often ludicrously moralistic history of
Japan written about the turn of this century, claimed that the
Sonshi, which was probably the best loved by the Japanese of the
Chinese military classics, contained 'not so much the principles
of war as the dirtiest form of statecraft with its unspeakable
depths of duplicity'. It was Murdoch's view that: 'The most
cynical, the very worst passages in the notorious Eighteenth
Chapter of "The Prince", pale before the naked and full-bodied
depravity of the old Chinese lore on espionage'.*

There is no question that the daimyos of this epoch were
obsessed with matters of espionage, infiltration, and subversion.

* James H. Murdoch. *A History of Japan*. Vol I. London: Kegan Paul, Trubner,
1910. P. 631.

left : An Ashikaga Shogun, one of the generalissmos who seized power in Japan during the fourteenth century in defiance of imperial authority.

below : Ashikaga Takauji.

above : Matsumoto Castle in the mountainous centre of Japan was built
in 1582 by the Ogasawara family. It is one of the few remaining castles
to have survived the civil wars and ravages of medieval Japan.

left : Toyotomi Hideyo:
the son of a peasant,
who overcame all
obstacles to become the
great unifier of
sixteenth–century
Japan.

These bellicose men were so intensely desirous of victory over
their rivals that they were willing to subordinate all else to the
pursuit of it. They condoned any means, no matter how decep-
tive, treacherous or callous, for the sake of victory. It seems in
fact to have been good form to 'do your dirtiest', as Murdoch
would have put it, to beat an enemy. One sixteenth century

Uesugi Kenshin holding a *gunpai*

European visitor to Japan commented, for example, that 'when
[the Japanese] wish to kill a person by treachery, they put on a
great pretence by entertaining him with every sign of love and
joy – and then in the middle of it all, off comes his head'.
    The daimyos lived in constant dread that their rivals might
develop techniques of espionage superior to their own. They
attempted, accordingly, to restrict all inter-domainal contacts
only to those that they could subject to the most rigorous

surveillance. Yet no matter how careful the daimyos were they could never be fully certain even of the loyalty of the officials who performed surveillance services for them. Frequently the daimyos felt obliged to assign as many spies to observe their own people close at hand as to undertake missions of information-gathering in enemy domains.

In their house laws the daimyos openly condoned the use of spies even during peacetime; and one has the impression that these *metsuke* ('eye-attachers') were at work everywhere. Some daimyos, who were especially beset by fears of subversion, even employed special spy-detectors (*meakashi* or 'eye-clearers') to ferret out *metsuke*. These spy-detectors were supposedly super-sleuths, who possessed extraordinary talents for uncovering disguises, spotting suspicious behaviour and so forth.

So conscious was everyone during the Provincial Wars epoch of the menace of spying that it was necessary for the daimyos to contrive ever more unusual ways of placing their undercover agents. One story, probably apocryphal, relates a subterfuge utilized by Hōjō Sōun, a daimyo who brought unity to the southern part of the Kantō about the turn of the sixteenth century. Sōun, according to the story, announced that all blind people under his governance were of utterly no use to him and, gathering together those in his castle town, he cast them into the sea. The other blind people of the domain immediately fled in search of sanctuary to nearby territories, where, of course, they covertly continued to operate as spies for their lord Sōun.

Although the Provincial Wars epoch with its spying and other cloak and dagger activities may have been an age of excitement and high adventure for men, at least within the samurai class, it was for women a time of pitiful decline. Aristocratic women earlier in Japanese history had enjoyed considerable social status and important economic rights, including the right to inherit property. But with the development and spread of feudalism, single-son inheritance (if not always primogeniture) came to be enforced by the typical samurai family to avoid division of its wealth and to maintain as far as possible family solidarity in the midst of highly competitive and predatory fighting conditions.

Not only were samurai women thus deprived of their former economic rights; owing to their physical frailty, they were held in increasingly lower social esteem by men whose chief, indeed almost sole, interest lay in the bearing of arms. The samurai of this era sought to acquire as their wives women who, socially and physically, could provide them with sturdy and distinguished male heirs.

Inasmuch as the samurai could presumably get all the illicit sex they wished from professional women and other amenable types they had scarcely any reason at all to consider the sentiment of romantic love in arranging their marriages. Moreover, if we are to believe the Jesuit missionaries of the sixteenth century who railed bitterly against 'the sin that does not bear mentioning', pederasty was widely practised among warriors. The Jesuits blamed what they regarded as the rampant homosexuality of the times in Japan chiefly on Buddhist priests, whom they charged with enjoying the love of young men so enormously themselves that they preached it as a positive virtue to others. It is probably also true, however, that the feudal lord-vassal tie in medieval Japan, as in medieval Europe, helped to stimulate the practice of homosexuality. Quite likely there were many samurai fighting men of this period who relied almost exclusively on their relationships with other males for the satisfaction of their emotional needs.

The stronger daimyos often dictated all samurai marriages within their domains. They tried to prohibit, or at least to restrict, marriages between their vassal families on the grounds that they might give rise to alliances that could threaten the daimyo houses themselves. On the other hand, the daimyos tended to use their own sisters, daughters and nieces – often in the most heartless fashion – as marriage pawns in their political and military manoeuvring with rival chieftains of other domains. One of the most pathetic victims of such matrimonial manoeuvring was Oichi, younger sister of the late sixteenth century unifier, Oda Nobunaga.

Oichi, who was regarded as a great beauty in her time, was first married by her brother to Nagamasa, son of the daimyo of the Asai family; and even though the marriage was arranged by

others, Oichi and her husband appear to have become genuinely
fond of each other. When Nobunaga finally decided to attack the
Asai in 1573 – probably to the surprise of no one, since the Oichi-
Nagamasa nuptials had been intended only to secure temporary
peace for both sides – Nagamasa sent his wife and three daughters
back to the Oda family. Having made this chivalrous gesture,
Nagamasa braced himself along with his kinsmen and allies for
Nobunaga's assault, an assault which resulted not only in
Nagamasa's own death but also in the permanent destruction of
the power of the Asai.

The victorious Nobunaga next gave Oichi in marriage to
Shibata Katsuie; and in 1583, when this daimyo was attacked
by Toyotomi Hideyoshi, Nobunaga's successor as military
hegemon of Japan, Shibata also tried to spare Oichi's life by
urging her to flee from his encampment. On this occasion, however, the lady refused and subsequently joined her second
husband in an act of double suicide when his forces were unable
successfully to withstand Hideyoshi's attack.

A revealing, although not entirely credible, story is told about
one of Nobunaga's own marriages. At the age of fifteen he was
wedded to Nōhime, ten-year-old daughter of the daimyo of the
neighbouring domain of Mino. After Nobunaga had succeeded
to his family's headship, Nōhime noticed that he began slipping
out of their bedroom for several hours each night. When she
asked his reason for doing this, Nobunaga, apparently in complete candour, told her that he had made an agreement with two
of her father's leading retainers to overthrow the Mino regime.
They were to kill her father on a night when the opportunity
presented itself and to signal Nobunaga by beacon-fire during a
specified interval of time after midnight. Nobunaga was then to
muster his troops and to invade Mino. Since he could not know
when the retainers would perform the assassination, Nobunaga
was obliged to get up each night to look for their signal. He
ended the conversation by reminding Nōhime that, as his wife,
she was duty-bound to speak of this matter to no one else.

At the time of her marriage Nōhime had in fact been entrusted
to spy on Nobunaga and she now duly relayed information of the
plot to her father, who promptly had the two accused retainers

put to death. Yet the truth was that the crafty Nobunaga had
fabricated the story precisely to bring about the execution of
these important lieutenants and thus to make the Mino domain
more vulnerable to attack.

A younger brother of the noted daimyo Takeda Shingen gave
what was probably the best marital advice to samurai of the

Takeda Shingen

Provincial Wars era in one of a set of injunctions he wrote for the
Takeda and their vassal families: 'The samurai must never relax
his guard. Even when alone with just his wife, he should not
forget to have his sword at hand.'

Of all the daimyos of this vigorous age, the awesomely
belligerent and indefatigable Takeda Shingen was the one who

perhaps most fully typified in his personal behaviour the particular samurai qualities that we have been discussing in this
chapter. Born in 1521 in the mountainous eastern domain of Kai,
Shingen learned the samurai skills at an early age – undoubtedly
with great relish and enthusiasm – and by his teens was already
campaigning with his father in other domains. Yet father and son
apparently shared no great love for each other; and in 1541, when
Shingen was only twenty, he suddenly drove his father out of
Kai and took the office of daimyo for himself.

Scholars have been at a loss to explain precisely why Shingen
turned on his father in this extraordinarily vicious way. Some
have suggested that he was forced to act as he did because of
pressures from certain Takeda vassals who strongly opposed his
father's conduct of domain affairs. Others have speculated that
the older Takeda deliberately had his son expel him so he could
seek shelter in a neighbouring domain and spy on its daimyo.
The latter hypothesis is rather far-fetched, especially since
Shingen's father was only forty-eight at the time and ultimately
spent the remainder of his long life until death at eighty-one
without ever being allowed to return to Kai.

Some years later, Shingen nearly suffered the same fate as his
father. This became clear in the disclosure in 1567 that his own
son was plotting rebellion against him with certain Takeda
vassals and people outside Kai. On this occasion, however,
Shingen the father moved first by incarcerating his son and later
forcing him to commit suicide. Shingen also pursued the initiative he had taken by having his vassals at the time sign a document swearing fidelity and loyal service to him and promising not
to join together in any future 'conspiratorial leagues'.

The drawing-up of oaths of loyalty and the like was common
among daimyos of this period who, it should be manifestly clear
by now, were able to trust no one. Of course such oaths and
pledges could easily be, and frequently were, broken by warriors
who valued professional success far more than the ethics of how
they achieved it. The daimyos accordingly often attempted to
insure that their pacts of vassal allegiance would be honoured by
making certain concessions in them, either in form or in actual
content. Mōri Motonari, daimyo of what was to become the great

Chōshū domain of western Honshu, for example, once had his sons and principal vassals sign their names around a circle drawn at the end of a pledge to abide by his military rules. The implication was that, for the purpose of this pledge at least, Motonari agreed to waive feudal, hierarchical distinctions and to grant his sons and followers an unprecedented equality of status with him.

The daimyos also tried to make the oaths and pledges they extracted from their vassals more binding by playing on the widely-held religious beliefs and fears of the age. In the above document that Shingen had his vassals sign, for instance, he inserted a clause stating that if any signatory should violate the vow he took he would not only incur the wrath of innumerable Shinto and Buddhist deities but would also be subjected to an attack of leprosy and would spend his life after death in eternal purgatory.

Even the strongest daimyos often had to use whatever means they could contrive to control their headstrong and vainglorious subordinates. Particularly delicate was the handling of personal fights or brawls among the latter, since they invariably either originated in or soon became inextricably enmeshed with questions of 'face' or honour. A common device for minimizing such fights and for avoiding the need to arbitrate them was the *ryō-seibai* or 'double guilt' doctrine, which many of the daimyos of the Provincial Wars period wrote into their house laws. According to this doctrine both parties to a fight, no matter what the issues involved or who started it, would be equally punishable. Often the death penalty was impossed on both antagonists, and a particularly diabolical way of implementing it was to have the men squat down facing each other and, at a signal, have each pierce the other's chest with a sword.

Many vassals strongly objected to the 'double guilt' doctrine and tried to resist its application. There is a story told that one of Shingen's vassals asserted his unwillingness to accept such a legal concept, which, according to him, would undermine the 'manly way' (*otoko no michi*) of the true samurai and would simply be a boon to cowards, who would henceforth be able to act as they wished and to insult whomever they pleased with impunity. If Shingen wanted his followers to maintain their properly aggressive spirit he had better find some other way to deal with squabbles among his retainers.

Inasmuch as Takeda Shingen was as ruthlessly aggressive as anyone during this age, he undoubtedly understood the sentiment that motivated this criticism. But he had the cold, hard task of suppressing disorder within his domain while conducting endless warfare against his foes outside it. He did not care to philosophize about the 'double guilt' doctrine or to assess it from the standpoint of right or wrong. As with everything else, if it suited his purpose and he could enforce it, he was little concerned with whether others liked it or not.

Shingen used as his military insignia a long, vertical banner emblazoned with the motto (taken from the *Sonshi*): 'fast as the wind; quiet as the forest; aggressive as fire; and immovable as a mountain'. Whatever the extent to which Shingen personally possessed these qualities, he was certainly one of the most vigorous and insatiable campaigners of the fighting scene in sixteenth-century Japan. His forces battled with those of his arch-rival, Uesugi Kenshin, on five separate occasions – in 1553, 1555, 1557, 1561 and 1564 – at Kawanakajima, located between Shingen's base province of Kai and Kenshin's domain on the Japan Sea coast of northern Honshu. Kenshin, who was as enthusiastic as Shingen in his love for combat, invaded the Kantō fourteen times over a twenty-seven year period; and on seven of these occasions he remained in the field for more than a year.

The Kawanakajima encounters brought no decisive benefit either to Takeda Shingen or Uesugi Kenshin, but the place itself as well as the linked names of these two warriors chieftains are, to the average Japanese even today, still evocative of the most tumultuous era in their country's history.

5
Trade, guns, and Christianity

The first Europeans to set foot on Japanese soil were Portuguese sailors who ran aground in a Chinese junk on the island of Tanegashima off the southern coast of Kyushu in or about 1542. During the ensuing century not only Portuguese, but also Spanish, Dutch and English among others, came to Japan and brought with them as their chief imports trade, guns and Christianity.

The Japanese were fascinated by the muzzle-loading muskets of the Portuguese and called them '*tanegashimas*' from the place where they first observed them; but guns, although employed in several key battles in the late sixteenth century, did not revolutionize warfare in Japan at this time. As already mentioned, the samurai of the thirteenth century were concerned chiefly with protecting the special warrior skills that set them off as a privileged ruling class, and had shown little interest in gunpowder even after its efficacy in battle had been demonstrated during the Mongol invasions. But by the late Provincial Wars epoch, warfare had become far more complex and competitive and the daimyos of this age could not afford to ignore the potential value to their armies of European-style guns and cannon. The problem was that these weapons were in very short supply; and by the time they became widely available about the turn of the seventeenth century, the imposition of a new military hegemony by the Tokugawa family brought warfare to an end in Japan.

Whatever the lasting historical influence of the Europeans who visited Japan during this pre-modern 'Christian century', they have left us a vast body of writings that provides innumerable and varied insights into Japanese life and customs of the times. As foreigners, the Europeans often noted and jotted down things that the Japanese themselves undoubtedly simply took for granted as too obvious to put in writing.

Among the earliest to record his observations of Japan and the Japanese was the great Jesuit father, St Francis Xavier, who spent the years 1549–51 in Japan. Xavier commented that:

> the people whom we have met so far are the best who have as yet been discovered, and it seems to me that we shall never find among the heathens another race to equal the Japanese . . . they are men of honour to a marvel, and prize honour above all else in the world . . . they highly regard arms and trust much therein; always carrying sword and dirk, both high and low alike, from the age of fourteen onwards.*

Accustomed though Xavier and his companions were to the tumult and violence of life in Europe at the dawn of its modern era, they could not resist remarking time and again on the extra-ordinarily martial temperament of the Japanese.

During the early part of their stay in Japan, the Europeans were confined in their activities largely to the western island of Kyushu. In 1550 Xavier journeyed to Kyoto in the hope of establishing the kind of ties with a central ruling body that the Jesuits usually regarded as essential for proselytizing effectively on a national scale. But he found the capital in such political turmoil that he soon despaired of achieving his purpose and returned to Kyushu, no doubt convinced that Japan was a hope-lessly disunited land.

In fact, Japan was far more advanced on the road to reunifica-tion than the Europeans at the time could have realized. There had come into being by the middle of the sixteenth century a number of highly autonomous and effectively controlled domains throughout the country that needed only a great leader to draw them together under unitary rule. The daimyos, sensing this and each aspiring to become the new military hegemon of the land, accelerated their campaigning and further enmeshed them-selves in marriage alliances, non-aggression pacts and the like.

* Quoted in C. R. Boxer. *The Christian Century in Japan, 1549–1650.* Berkeley and Los Angeles: University of California Press, 1967. P. 401.

The chieftain who eventually took the first truly significant steps towards reunifying the country was Oda Nobunaga, daimyo of the province of Owari midway between the Kansai and the Kantō. In 1560 Nobunaga won a spectacular victory against a powerful neighbour and began a sustained drive that within eight years of hard combat led him triumphantly into Kyoto, the ancient seat of imperial authority, which was both the sentimental goal of all aspirant unifiers and the central base from which Nobunaga planned to implement his motto of *tenka fubu* – 'All the country under [my] military control'. During the next decade and a half, until his death in 1582, Nobunaga pursued his campaigns of conquest outward from Kyoto; in the process he liquidated the Ashikaga Shogunate and made himself, in name as well as in fact, the new military dictator of nearly half of Japan.

The Jesuit fathers who personally met Nobunaga have left a number of quite favourable impressions, picturing him as a man of resolution and action, sensitive to honour, who was well suited to the task of reinstating order in Japan. Although they did not ignore his darker side, the Jesuits were understandably biased in their views of Nobunaga. For the latter, who had an intense hatred of certain powerful Buddhist temples and sects that opposed his pursuit of military reunification, openly encouraged the activities of the foreign Christians in order to undermine Buddhist influence in general in Japan. The fact is that Nobunaga was a man of exceptional brutality even in a brutal age, and later historians, shocked by the sheer enormity of his atrocities, have on the whole not regarded him charitably. The distinguished Western scholar of Japan, Sir George Sansom, has for example asserted emphatically of Nobunaga that: 'His vindictive ruthlessness is apparent from the beginning of his career . . . to his last years, which were filled with wanton slaughter. He became the master of twenty provinces at a terrible cost. He was a cruel and callous brute'.*

Perhaps the most dramatic and notoriously memorable of Nobunaga's 'war crimes' was his attack on the complex of buildings, situated atop Mount Hiei to the northeast of Kyoto, that

* George Sansom. *A History of Japan, 1334–1615*. Stanford: Stanford University Press, 1961. P. 310.

constituted the Enryakuji temple, which for more than seven and a half centuries had served as the greatest centre of Buddhist study and training in Japan. Since the Enryakuji was at this time openly allied with Nobunaga's enemies, it was a legitimate target of attack. But Nobunaga was not content to punish it with a simple or conventional punitive action; instead he determined to destroy the Enryakuji completely. In the autumn of 1571 his men surrounded Mount Hiei and marched up its sides, burning every building they found and slaughtering some three thousand people, including not only monks but also men, women and children who had gathered there from nearby villages. It is said that not a single plea for mercy was heeded during this awful act of blood-letting and that the corpses came to fill every 'hill and valley' of Mount Hiei.

Apart from his unquestioned personal cruelty, Nobunaga was in many ways a very progressive military leader for his day. As one of the first to recognize the value of firearms, he moved quickly to control the few centres for their production in the central provinces. In an epochal battle with the forces of the Takeda in 1575, Nobunaga convincingly demonstrated the superiority of guns over mounted samurai. The mighty Shingen had died two years earlier and the Takeda were at the time under the command of his less distinguished son. A contemporary screen-painting shows in vivid detail how the Takeda horsemen charged against the zigzagged rows of posts that Nobunaga erected and from behind which his infantry, armed with about three thousand muskets, shot them down at close range.

Nobunaga, who lived by the sword, died by it in 1582 at the age of forty-nine. When one of his generals, Akechi Mitsuhide, surrounded and attacked the temple building in Kyoto where Nobunaga, with a small retinue was lodging, for the night. In the course of fighting the temple was burned down and Nobunaga's body was never found. It is said that he cut open his belly and deliberately set fire to the building to avoid the indignity – to which he had subjected countless numbers of his enemies – of being publicly displayed in death.

Nobunaga's avenger was another of his generals, Toyotomi Hideyoshi, who at the time of Mitsuhide's treachery was campaigning in the western provinces of Honshu. Hideyoshi had recently won an important victory in the siege of a castle stronghold at Tottori, an undertaking which he began only after buying up at double the price all the available rice in the surrounding vicinity and thereby preventing the defenders from laying in an adequate supply of food. Sieging was not an easy business in sixteenth century Japan. In the absence of cannonry sufficient to

Oda Nobunaga

destroy heavy stone and mortar defence works, besieging armies could find themselves stalemated indefinitely by well-stocked and determined bands of men. It therefore required the imagination and skill of a Hideyoshi to be consistently superior in this kind of warfare.

When Hideyoshi received word of Nobunaga's assassination, he was in the process of flooding-out or 'drowning' another great fortress – this one at Takamatsu – by erecting dykes and by diverting huge volumes of both river and rain water into them. Promptly arranging a truce with the Takamatsu defenders (who were ignorant of the assassination), he now marched rapidly back to the central provinces and at one stroke destroyed Mitsuhide.

In a few weeks of breath-taking events Hideyoshi thus emerged as the new hegemon of Japan and found himself in a position to complete the task of unification begun by Nobunaga. During the next eight years Hideyoshi, commonly regarded as the greatest military commander in Japanese history, marched from one end of the country to the other to impose his rule through a combination of force and diplomatic persuasion, the latter a technique unknown to Nobunaga. By 1590 no other daimyo dared challenge him further and Hideyoshi, operating chiefly from his castle headquarters in Osaka, exercised greater control over the land than anyone previously in Japanese history.

Hideyoshi and Akechi Mitsuhide were of a considerably different social type from the samurai leaders of several centuries earlier in Japanese history or even the relatively upstart (*gekokujō*) daimyos of the period following the Ōnin War; for these men rose swiftly from the very ranks of the peasantry to the heights of military power. Combined with important factors in the evolution of warfare at this time – such as the expanding use of infantry troops and firearms – their kind of social ascent would no doubt soon have brought the break-up of the samurai as a privileged arms-bearing élite, just as the development of modern warfare had dissolved the knightly class of Europe at the end of the Middle Ages. Yet Hideyoshi himself began a series of measures which, as continued by the Tokugawa after him, drew a sharp distinction between the samurai and other classes and insured the former's ruling dominance for at least another two and a half centuries.

The most important of these measures was the great 'sword hunt' of 1588, by means of which Hideyoshi sought to render the peasantry militarily neutral through the wholesale confiscation of its weapons. He followed this up with decrees instructing farmers to remain, unarmed, in the countryside, and samurai to reside permanently in the castle towns under the direct jurisdiction of their daimyos. Neither samurai nor peasants, moreover, were to intermingle with artisans and merchants, the other two major classes of Japanese society.

Although generally shrewd and carefully calculating in his ways, Hideyoshi was responsible in his later years for two terrible follies in the unsuccessful Japanese attempts to invade Korea in 1592 and 1597. These huge undertakings, which involved about a hundred and sixty thousand expeditionary troops the first time and a hundred and forty thousand the second, may have been partly motivated by Hideyoshi's desire to expand overseas trading operations through force. Yet it is also entirely possible that Hideyoshi, who did not actually accompany the invading armies, simply suffered from the same kind of mania to conquer for conquering's sake that has afflicted so many autocratic rulers in world history, including Khubilai Khan during the thirteenth century.

One point about the invasions worthy of note is that they were the only instances in the thousand-year history of the samurai class in pre-modern times that Japanese soldiers came to venture aggressively abroad. Despite their undeniably strong militaristic tradition, the Japanese have, until the modern era, been conspicuously less imperialistic in their behaviour than any other major race of people in the world.

When Hideyoshi died in 1598 he left as his successor a young child of five, a fact that set in motion a process of manoeuvring for power among the great daimyos which resulted in the decisive victory of Tokugawa Ieyasu at the battle of Sekigahara in 1600.

Ieyasu, whose domain was in the Kantō with its castle town at Edo (present-day Tokyo), assumed the title of shogun in 1603 and imposed upon Japan a governing system that endured for two and a half centuries and provided one of the longest periods of almost uninterrupted peace in the history of any country of the world. What Ieyasu and his immediate successors did was to finalize the arrangement of national order on the basis of daimyo domains that had been taking shape in Japan for nearly a century. Like Hideyoshi before him, Ieyasu did not seek to conquer the country completely; rather, he was content to allow the various daimyos to retain almost complete autonomy over the internal

affairs of their domains so long as each vowed lasting allegiance
to the Tokugawa house.

Ieyasu and his successors also employed a variety of devices
that had been evolved during the Provincial Wars epoch as means
for controlling their vassals. By shifting certain daimyos from
one domain to another, they sought so far as possible to inter-
sperse friendly lords among those less favourably inclined
towards the Tokugawa house and thus to reduce the likelihood
of the formation of hostile territorial leagues. They also forbade
marriages between the daimyo families without express shogunate approval and ordered the destruction of all castles except
one in each domain.

But perhaps the most important institution that the Tokugawa
adopted to ensure their continued hegemony of the land was the
system of hostages and compulsory attendance at Edo which
they required of the daimyos and their families. The exchange of
hostages to seal pacts and to strengthen 'loyalty' arrangements
had been common practice throughout the sixteenth century.
Ieyasu himself had spent many of his childhood years as a hostage of first one and then the other of his father's two most
threatening neighbours, the Oda and Imagawa families. And
Hideyoshi, even after assuming national power, had allowed
Ieyasu to hold his mother as hostage to allay the latter chieftain's
fears that Hideyoshi might decide to violate the uneasy truce that
existed between them.

Under the Tokugawa Shogunate the daimyos were, with few
exceptions, required to leave their wives and children permanently
in Edo. Moreover, they were personally obliged to spend a
specified period of each year in attendance at the shogunate
court. In this way the daimyos and their retinues were kept
shuffling back and forth between their domains and Edo, with
the double advantage to the shogunate that they could be
regularly observed and could also be held absent from their
domains sufficiently frequently to make difficult their participa-
tion in any local plots or subversion.

Although the Tokugawa ruling system was the carefully con-
structed end-product of a long period of institutional growth, its
extraordinary longevity was ultimately made possible by the

top : The Great Revenge: after years of waiting and preparation the forty-seven *rōnin* mount their successful attack on Lord Kira's mansion.

bottom : Retribution: the killing of Lord Kira.

Members of the loyal league of *rōnin* who attacked and killed Lord Kira. Their names appear next to their portraits.

The end of a samurai: the warrior and his sword are finally destroyed by gunpowder.

policy of national seclusion which the shogunate adopted shortly before the middle of the seventeenth century. All Japanese were at this time permanently prohibited from leaving the country and all outsiders were denied permission to visit it with the exception of a small number of Chinese and Dutch traders at Nagasaki. By means of the seclusion policy the Tokugawa regime was able to proscribe Christianity, which it had come to fear almost hysterically as a threat to Japanese social values, and to control foreign trade. But perhaps most important for the long-term continuance of its rule, the shogunate was able to restrict to a virtual minimum the presence of foreigners in Kyushu, which contained the domains of several daimyos who had been among Ieyasu's most formidable opponents at Sekigahara and who might well have sought to ally themselves militarily with the Europeans against Edo.

The samurai occupied an anomolous position in isolated Japan of Tokugawa times. These warriors, who along with their families constituted between seven and ten per cent of the national population, were guaranteed superior social prerogatives and hereditary stipends by the statutes of both Hideyoshi and the Tokugawa. They alone, moreover, enjoyed the privilege of wearing swords, the visible symbols of their ascendant rank, and had the theoretical (although presumably seldom exercised) right to cut down any member of another class who chanced to offend or displease them. Yet, whatever their special rights and privileges, the samurai of this age were in fact warriors who had no wars to fight. Unable to pursue the profession that supposedly justified their existence, they were obliged to seek employment in other fields – such as government or teaching – or simply to remain idle and attempt to get by on their stipends, which in nearly all cases were either held constant or were reduced while prices rose steadily.

Nevertheless it appears to have been precisely because they were unable to engage in warfare that the samurai of this era became particularly self-conscious of themselves as a class and of their unique role in Japanese history. They came, for example, to romanticize the deeds and behaviour of their ancestors, to find all glory and manliness in the conduct of earlier samurai

7

even when that conduct had obviously sprung from the most savage emotions.

In addition, the Tokugawa period samurai, who used their leisure to acquire a degree of education unknown among fighting men of earlier times, sought collectively to form an ideal code of behaviour for themselves. This code, which is generally known as *bushidō* or the way of the *bushi* (an alternate term for samurai), cannot be defined in a few words. Like any code of social ethics,

Sketch of a samurai by Kuniyoshi, late Tokugawa period

it has been subjected to innumerable shadings of interpretation. Yet at the core of *bushidō* in the Tokugawa era was the belief that the samurai owed absolute devotion to their feudal overlords, a devotion that contrasted sharply with the often opportunistic 'loyalty' – which could be turned in an instant to betrayal – that had prevailed widely in the Provincial Wars epoch. In this later age the samurai did not have to test their devotion or loyalty on a day-to-day basis in the rigours of warfare and rapidly changing fortunes, but could enshrine it as an ultimate moral standard for the overall conduct of their lives.

The nature of Tokugawa loyalty as it ideally functioned under the code of *bushidō* can nowhere be seen better than in the stirring incident of the revenge of the forty-seven *rōnin*, or 'masterless samurai', that occurred in the early years of the eighteenth century.

It was the custom of the Tokugawa shogunate to impose on certain daimyos the responsibility for financing and handling the reception of envoys from the imperial court when they visited Edo, a responsibility that in 1701 fell to Lord Asano of the western domain of Akō. In order to handle properly the intricate matters of ceremonial that were required on such an occasion, Lord Asano placed himself, shortly after his arrival in Edo, under the tutelage of one of the shogunate's chiefs of protocol, a man named Kira. It is not clear precisely what happened between Asano and Kira, but soon the former came to feel that he had been deeply offended. Perhaps it was due to an insult made by Kira (whom Murdoch claims had a 'most pronounced itch in his palm') because Lord Asano failed to give him suitable presents for the services he rendered. Whatever the cause, Asano one morning suddenly attacked Kira with his sword, hacking him severely on the shoulder and forehead before the two were separated by others nearby.

Asano, although he acted in the true samurai spirit, had committed the grave offence – punishable by death – of drawing his sword in the shogunate palace. Officials were accordingly sent to his apartment that very afternoon to inform him that he must forthwith perform *seppuku*. Apparently the shogun ordered Asano's *seppuku* immediately to spare him from learning that

Kira did not die from his wounds, but would survive. In any event Asano committed suicide that evening on a hastily arranged dais of mats and was buried a few hours later at the Sengakuji temple in Edo.

When word of Asano's death was carried back to Akō by special couriers, his retainers, headed by Ōishi Kuranosuke, were thunderstruck, and in their initial excitement proposed a variety of courses of action from committing mass suicide instantly to undertaking a commando raid on Kira's house in Edo. Presently, however, reason prevailed and the Asano retainers decided to await more detailed information of the incident. They were in general agreement that they should concentrate their efforts primarily on seeking to persuade the shogunate not to confiscate the Akō domain, as it was likely to do, but allow Asano's younger brother to succeed to its headship.

More than a year passed before the shogunate finally decreed that the Asano family must forfeit Akō. In so doing it also automatically reduced all of the Asano retainers to the status of *rōnin*. Freed from the need to wait further for official leniency, a group of the latter – originally numbering over one hundred but later reduced to forty-seven – now formed a secret pact to avenge their dead lord through the assassination of Kira.

Legend has it that several of the forty-seven *rōnin* went to great lengths to make it appear that they were no longer concerned with the tragedy that had befallen the house of Asano, but wished henceforth only to be allowed to live as peacefully and pleasurably as possible. Ōishi Kuranosuke, who actually did leave his wife and children, is invariably shown in fictionalized versions of this story leading a life of drunkenness and dissipation in brothels and wine houses as he and the others awaited their opportunity to strike.

The attack on Kira finally took place on 14 December – the same day of the month that Lord Asano had died – in the year of 1702. Cutting down the few attendants who tried to block their way into his residence, the *rōnin* entered en masse and, after a rather frantic search, found Kira hiding in a coal shed and killed him. Later that night they took his head to the Sengakuji temple, placed it on Asano's grave and, upon completion of this solemn and highly symbolic act of vengeance fulfilled, surrendered themselves to the Edo authorities.

The public outburst of sympathy and admiration for the forty-seven *rōnin* was immediate and virtually unanimous. Even among a number of the shogunate officialdom there was a widespread desire to exonerate them. Yet the *rōnin* had broken fundamental Tokugawa laws aimed at the maintenance of peace and, after a period of a few months of hesitation, they were directed to disembowel themselves. It is significant to note, as an indication of the attitudes of the time, however, that the estates of Kira's grandson and successor were at the same time confiscated on the grounds that, although he had been wounded in the attack of the *rōnin*, he had failed to fight to the death in defence of his grandfather.

In their martyrdom, Ōishi Kuranosuke and the other members of the band of forty-seven *rōnin* achieved a folk immortality that can be matched by few others in Japan's history. Their story, which has been rendered as *Chūshingura* ('A Treasury of Loyal Hearts') in every imaginable medium of the performing arts, including the puppet and Kabuki theatres and, of course, the cinema, is simply without challenge the most overwhelmingly popular of all among Japanese audiences. By their noble conduct they bequeathed to all later generations an example of the spirit of the pre-modern samurai at its best.

Epilogue

The arrival of Commodore Matthew Perry of the United States and his 'black ships' in Japanese waters in 1853 forced Japan to abandon its seclusion policy of more than two centuries and inaugurated a decade and a half of domestic and foreign crisis which the Tokugawa Shogunate, excessively weighted by tradition, showed itself increasingly unable to handle. In the end a group of lower-ranking samurai, led by those from certain particularly powerful domains in the west, proclaimed the shogunate an unworthy governing body, and in 1867 overthrew it with the

Idealization of the samurai, by Hokusai

stated aim of restoring the emperor, long a shadowy figure in Kyoto under the Tokugawa hegemony, to his 'rightful' position of ruling authority.

In the process of destroying the Tokugawa Shogunate these activist samurai led Japan into the modern world, although few of them at the time had any real idea of the sweeping changes this would bring. Imperial loyalism provided a priceless means for overcoming the particularized type of devotion to feudal overlord that had been the social norm during the Tokugawa period. With the emperor to serve as a refurbished symbol of loyalty and devotion for all the Japanese people the inculcation of a true spirit of modern nationalism was made possible.

Yet real governing power was not restored to the throne. Instead, it was assumed by a small group of men, composed chiefly of activist samurai, who became an enlightened oligarchy dedicated to transforming Japan into a strong modern nation on European and American lines. Although they made every effort to encourage other samurai to become the leaders of the new Japan as they had been of the old, the oligarchs soon realized that the retention of an hereditary and privileged warrior class was incompatible with the needs of a modern society. Hence in the early 1870s they abolished the special rights of the samurai and decreed broad social and legal equality for the mass of the Japanese people.

Thus the samurai as a clearly identifiable class were eliminated from history. But the moral values and standards of behaviour embodied in the 'way of the samurai' remained, for better or worse, among the most powerful of guides for the Japanese as they progressed into the twentieth century.

Notes on further reading

Inasmuch as the samurai were the ruling class of Japan from the end of the twelfth century until the beginning of the modern era, their record constitutes the main theme of Japanese history during this period. Probably the best general treatments of samurai affairs during these centuries are to be found in Sir George Sansom's *A History of Japan*, three volumes (Stanford: Stanford University Press, 1958–63. Also in paperback) and the Japan portions of the two-volume *History of East Asian Civilization* (Boston: Houghton Mifflin, 1958–65) by Edwin O. Reischauer, John K. Fairbank and Albert M. Craig.

An excellent study of the rise of the samurai to national power may be found in Minoru Shinoda's *The Founding of the Kamakura Shogunate*, 1180–85 (New York: Columbia University Press, 1960): and *The Ōnin War* (New York: Columbia University Press, 1967) by H. Paul Varley presents a survey of institutional developments in warrior society during the first three centuries of the medieval age. Finally, Conrad D. Totman's *Politics in the Tokugawa Bakufu*, 1600–1843 (Cambridge: Harvard University Press, 1967) deals with politics during the final stage of the development of the samurai as a ruling class.

For those interested in a general analysis of the attitudes and behaviour of the modern Japanese, many of which derive directly from the samurai heritage, Ruth F. Benedict's *The Chrysanthemum and the Sword: Patterns of Japanese Culture* (Boston: Houghton Mifflin, 1946. Tuttle paperback) still makes fascinating, if somewhat dated, reading.

Map of Japan

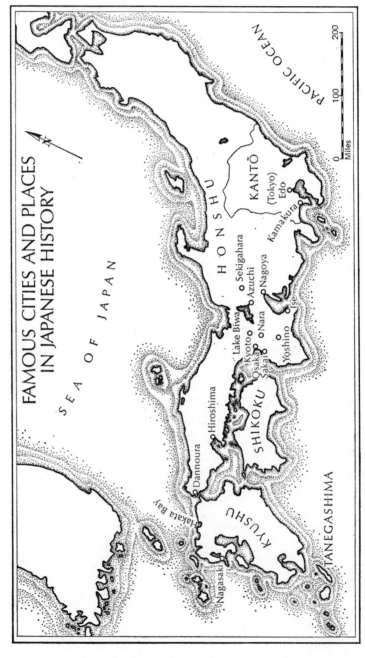

FAMOUS CITIES AND PLACES
IN JAPANESE HISTORY

SEA OF JAPAN

PACIFIC OCEAN

HONSHU

KANTŌ

(Tokyo)
Edo

Kamakura

Sekigahara
Azuchi

Nagoya

Lake Biwa

Kyoto
Nara

Osaka
Sakai

Yoshino

SHIKOKU

Hiroshima

Dannoura

Hakata Bay

KYUSHU

Nagasaki

TANEGASHIMA

0   100   200
Miles

Chronology

1600–1867	TOKUGAWA PERIOD
1701–1702	Incident of Revenge of Forty-seven Rōnin
1853	Perry's Arrival in Japan
1868	MEIJI RESTORATION
1873–1876	Abolition of Samurai Class

Index